WARTIME IS *YOU*

To l-
wi l-

'/ation

" 'Wartime is *Your* Time' is a book chronicling the lives of women during the First World War, while their men were fighting at the front.

They left their home comforts and took over men's jobs, with great success. They worked on the land, in munitions factories, as VAD's and ambulance drivers at the Front. Often they too lost their lives in this way.

My book illustrates their experiences, with photographs and memories. These are interwoven with magazine articles and background discussion, through a number of books. Some of these offer explanations for the continuing success of the magazines up to and including the present day, picturing a world that is often far removed from reality.

Marian Gold

WARTIME IS *YOUR* TIME

Women's Lives in World War I

Women's Image in the Magazines
compared with the reality of their Wartime Lives

by

MARIAN GOLD

SMOKING GUN BOOKS LTD

A SMOKING GUN BOOK

Published in Great Britain by Smoking Gun Books Ltd
2009

ISBN 09552661-4-0

SMOKING GUN BOOKS LTD
1 Golfside Close London N20 0RD

1914

"We have become too comfortable, too indulgent, many perhaps too selfish. And the stern hand of fate has scourged us to an elevation where we can see the great everlasting things that matter for a nation, the great peaks of honour, duty and patriotism, glad in glittering white, the great pinnacle of sacrifice pointing like a rugged finger to heaven" RT.HON.LLOYD GEORGE, September 19th 1914   (Painted specially for this work by Harold Coping)

"When the Vision dies in the dust of the market place,
When the Light is dim,
When you lift up your eyes and cannot behold his face,
When your heart is far from him,

Know this is your War; in this loneliest hour you ride
Down the roads he knew;
Though he comes no more at night he will kneel at your side
For comfort to dream with you."

                                        May Wedderburn Cannan

Drawn by Paul Thiriat.

The Last Token of
Esteem to the Fallen.

CONTENTS

I left school at fourteen, further education not being financially available. I experienced an awakened need to continue my education for many years; seeing the opportunities available to my children, I decided to take an 'A' level with a close friend, who was terminally ill, because I wished to support and encourage her.

In 1979 I joined the 'Fresh Horizons' Course at the City Lit. in Malet Street, as a preparation for a degree course. We studied English, History and the art of essay writing. In 1980 I decided to take the contemporary Studies B.A. (Hons.) Degree at Hatfield Polytechnic, majoring in English Literature. My children were by then having essay crises - why shouldn't I? During the final year of my degree I also helped to organise and run the Educational Guidance Centre at Hatfield Polytechnic. This unit was set up to assist people to return to study or retrain and rethink their careers.

The friends I had made at 'Fresh Horizons' became the nucleus of a group of mature students at Hatfield. We helped each other throughout the four year course, continuing to look after our children and run our homes *almost* as efficiently as before. I graduated with a 2.1 in 1984. Then I attended a one year Introductory Counselling Course at Hatfield Polytechnic.

I joined the M.A. degree course in 1986, as it was a two year intake. It was a two year taught, one year dissertation course: 'Literature In Crisis'. Most of the second year was based on the study of the literature of the First World War. The horrors of that war were more closely brought home to me when I went with some of my fellow students to the battlefields of Northern France. During this visit, we spent some time in a museum which had become the lifelong passion of one man. He had been collecting war memorabilia for over seventy years, and still continued unearthing relics in the fields around the museum. This museum, and his work, was the main inspiration for my idea for the dissertation, which grew out of the emotion that had been aroused in me by this particular part of the course.

MARIAN GOLD M.A.

ACKNOWLEDGEMENTS

I would like to thank the following people for their support, help and encouragement: Dr Gill Davies, Head of English Department, Edge Hill University College; my husband, Conrad Gold; all my family; and my many patient friends who have always been ready to help and listen.

CHRONOLOGY

1914:

28th June	Assassination of the heir to the Austro-Hungarian Empire, the Archduke Franz Ferdinand and his wife in Sarajevo, by the Bosnian student Princip, who was under orders from the secret 'Black Hand' Organisation (there was no direct involvement by the Serbian Government).
23rd July	Austro-Hungarian Note presented to Serbia.
28th July	Austria-Hungary declares war on Serbia.
31st July	Russia orders general mobilisation.
July	212,000 women employed in Britain in what were to become the munitions industries. Messages between Tsar, Kaiser and King George.
1st August	German mobilisation ordered. Germany declares war on Russia. German troops invade Luxembourg. France mobilises.
2nd August	German troops enter French territory. Russian troops cross German frontier.
3rd August	British Fleet mobilised. Invasion of Belgium by German army.
4th August	Germany declares war on France and also on Belgium. British army mobilises. Britain's ultimatum to Germany. Sir Edward Grey, British Foreign Secretary: "The lamps are going out all over Europe; we shall not see them lit again in our lifetime."
5th August	Britain declares war on Germany. Railways commandeered.

6th August	Lord Kitchener becomes Secretary for War. Austria declares war on Russia.
8th August	DORA (Defence of the Realm Act) introduced. Any government acquired wide powers to issue regulations affecting armed forces and civilians alike. Virtually all powers, other than that of taxation, were concentrated in the executive.
10th August	War declared on Austria-Hungary by France.
13th August	War declared on Austria by Great Britain.
15th August	Japanese ultimatum to Germany. Opening of the Panama Canal. This event, which in the ordinary course would have claimed universal attention in England, passed almost unnoticed in the press.
17th August	"The Expeditionary Force, as detailed for foreign service, has been safely landed on French soil. The embarkation, transportation and disembarkation of men and stores were alike carried through with the greatest possible precision and without a single casualty". This was the first intimation that British soldiers were on the Continent. The whole proceeding had passed without comment in the press, who had loyally supported Lord Kitchener in abstaining from printing the news, of which they were probably in possession.
19th September	"We have been too comfortable, too indulgent, many perhaps too selfish. And the stern hand of fate has scourged us to an elevation where we can see the great everlasting things that matter for a nation, the great peaks of honour, duty and patriotism, clad in glittering white, the great pinnacle of sacrifice pointing like a rugged finger to Heaven." RT HON. D LLOYD GEORGE.
19th October	Sir John French issues despatch dealing with the Battles of the Marne and the Aisne. In the latter the British losses were 561 officers and 12,980 men killed, wounded and missing.

December	The original British Expeditionary Force had already suffered 90% casualties.

1915:

	During 1915, the British Army in France suffered 300,000 casualties.
February	Flour cost 75% more than a year before, meat was up by 12%, coal by 15% and sugar 72%: 'Labour members in Parliament stated that many labourers were getting only one good meal a week; they did not say whether the labourers' wives or children were getting even that.'
February	The Germans declared the western approaches to the British isles to be a zone of war, into which neutral vessels entered at the risk of being sunk by German mines or submarines.
April	Britain had stores of food to last only six weeks. By adopting rationing of essentials, and by real deprivation, this proved just enough.
April	'Discovery' of 'War Babies'. In a letter to the Morning Post, a Conservative MP announced that throughout the country, in districts where large numbers of troops had been quartered, a 'great number of girls' were about to become unmarried mothers.
17th April	First Zeppelin raids – Newcastle, Maldon Shorncliffe and Lowestoft.
June	A Zeppelin raid in Hull. The Germans dropped thirteen high explosive and thirty-nine incendiary bombs, killing twenty-four people and injuring forty.
11th June	Kitchener drowned. A week after the Battle of Jutland, on his way to Russia in the cruiser Hampshire, Lord Kitchener was killed when it struck a mine off the Orkneys.

15th July	National Register of all persons, male or female, aged between 15 and 65 – the forerunner of conscription.
17th July	Rally organised by WSPU (Women's Social and Political Union) on behalf of women's 'Right to Serve'.
July	256,000 women now employed in the munitions industries.

1916:

March	Any woman or girl over school-leaving age who had worked on the land for not less than thirty days since the commencement of the War, was awarded the armlet of green baize, bearing a red crown, by the President of the Board of Agriculture. The certificate issued with the armlet stated: 'Every woman who helps in agriculture during the war is as truly serving her country as the man who is fighting in the trenches, on the sea, or in the air.'
May	Introduction of conscription. By then, between 2 and 3 million men had been recruited.
1st July	In a single day's battle which opened the Allied offensive on the Somme, the British Army endured a further 60,000 casualties, of whom one-third were killed.
4th July	The beginning of the immense convoys of casualties which came without cessation for about a fortnight after the Battle of the Somme and continued at short intervals for the whole of July and the first part of August.
July	520,000 women now employed in the munitions industries – an increase of over 100 per cent from 1915.

September	The War Office paid women the compliment that they had shown themselves capable of replacing the stronger sex in practically every calling.
	The Chief Factory Inspector, in his report for 1916, referred to the 'new self-confidence engendered in women' by the new conditions of work.
December	Ministry of Food established.

1917:

At Passchendaele, the British advanced five miles at a cost of 400,000 men.

Eleanor Rathbone, a leading feminist, established the Family Endowment Council to lead a fight for family allowances. She called for a weekly payment of 12s 6d for wives, plus 5s for the first child and 3s 6d for subsequent children, to be paid directly to the wives.

February	The total number of bus conductresses leapt from the handful of the previous year to about 2,500, some half of whom were former domestic servants.
3rd February	Voluntary rationing. Each citizen was to restrict himself to 4lbs of bread or 3lbs of flour, 2½lbs of meat and ¾ 1b of sugar per week.
March	Women enrolled in the Land Army could expect to receive a minimum wage of 18s per week, rising to 20s after three months, with an extra 2s 6d possible after a further three months' service.
6th April	United States declared war on Germany.
13th June	The worst bombing raid of the war: 162 people killed and 432 injured.
July	There were now 45,000 women in nursing.
August	Manpower finally treated as one whole source of effort, to be recruited for either factories or forces under a single Ministry of National Service.
December	United States declared war on Austria.

With Britain only three weeks from starvation, food rationing was finally introduced.

10th December — *The Times* listed the following as in short supply in London: sugar, tea, butter, margarine, lard, dripping, milk, bacon, pork, condensed milk, rice, currants, raisins, spirits.

1918:

29th January — The *Landswoman* magazine: A rally to overcome prejudice: 'The procession attracted much attention, and to many of the watchers it was a novelty to see the girls in their working clothes, and to realise that the girls of England are really working on the land, and not merely playing about in print frocks at haymaking time.'

6th February — Representation of the People Act gave women of thirty and over the vote on the same terms as men; a year later, the Sex Disqualification (Removal) Act made it law that women could no longer be barred from pursuing any profession or holding any office simply because of their sex or marital status. Thus women's suffrage became a part of English law, creeping in with an incongruous irony in the deepest time of wartime depression.

11th April — Sir Douglas Haig's 'Special Order of the Day':

"There is no course open to us but to fight it out. Every position must be held to the last man: there must be no retirement. With our backs to the wall and believing in the justice of our cause, each one of us must fight on to the end. The safety of our homes and the freedom of mankind alike depend upon the conduct of each one of us at this critical moment."

20th April — The Great London Rally. Over 200 land women, headed by the band of the 17th Battalion London Regiment, and accompanied by flower-decked wagons, together with pigs, lambs and ducks, marched through the streets of the West End and held a recruiting demonstration in Hyde Park – as a result of the Rally 1,000 girls enrolled in the Land Army.

Summer

The great influenza epidemic, which had struck Britain by this time, reached its height by the end of the year, and produced a new outbreak during the first three months of 1919. Coming at this time, it added greatly to human misery. In England and Wales 150,000 people died of it, more than 15,000 of them in London alone.

11th November

Armistice Day. When the sound of victorious guns burst over London at 11 a.m., the men and women who looked incredulously into each other's faces did not cry jubilantly, "We've won the War!" They only said, "The War is over."

30th November

The Women's Land Army demobilised.

November

Vogue magazine: 'For many women the end of the war must necessarily imply the closing of a stimulating chapter of experiences... Many a chauffeuse in navy blue or military khaki will regret the Mercedes in which she came to have almost a proprietary interest... To many, the War has brought responsibility and conspicuous service.'

INTRODUCTION

The purpose of this book is to look at a particular and very important historical period - The First World War - from the point of view of women, and by examining the magazines they read. This was a time of enormous upheaval at home, to a greater extent than any previous war, and was instrumental in bringing great social changes to the fore. The study of women's magazines reveals how they used their contents to discuss changing attitudes, morals and manners, while retaining certain themes, values and goals, by selective filtering and interpretation of aspects of 'the world'. There will also be discussion of how effective the magazines' influence was on the women who read them, as well as to note their effect in being seen as an ephemeral part of their lives.

Although there was - and still is - a general similarity of format within most women's magazines in terms of stories, articles, letters and advice pages, the editorial voice in wartime maintained absences and contradictions which bore little resemblance to the true situation of many of their women readers. Furthermore, some of the recently re-published women's literature, as well as the novels, plays and poetry already in print, show an entirely different world from that of the magazines. By their very nature, the magazines were, therefore, difficult to use as evidence of women's lives at the time under discussion.

This book will look at these contradictions, through the ways in which women's lives were represented in magazines and literature. In addition, it has, fortunately, been possible to draw on the experiences of a cross section of women whose memories have been incorporated.

In the magazines, even the war became domesticated: not soldiers dying in the trenches; nurses being bombed as they tended the wounded, and female ambulance drivers being shelled while driving the pathetic remnants of 'glorious manhood' to hospitals. Other than in one magazine - *The Englishwoman* - no major political issues of the day were discussed. In *My Weekly*, for example, there was the following discussion on "How to make the boys 'Fond'":

"Now, my dear girl, there are scores of sweet girls in England and Scotland who have never met a man who was worth liking. For goodness sake, don't choose your sweethearts until you have met plenty of men. If you do, the chances are both your courtship and your marriage will be miserable failures... Let your conversation be merry and interesting, not frivolous to the point of silliness, and your temper kindly... you will soon have every nice fellow of your acquaintance speaking of you as 'one of the sweetest girls I know'."

Popular literature, such as romantic novels and women's magazines, constructs a world revolving around women's domestic lives. This type of writing would seem both to reflect and influence the roles that women play in real life. Women's magazines are now being seen as having an important contribution to offer to the study of women's position in society, both past and present. They draw on a relationship between a popular form and its readers. They provide a long standing public record of women's lives and experiences, reflecting and helping to shape both a woman's view of herself and society's view of her. Remarkably, in spite of the fact that the lives of their readers have undergone enormous social and political changes, the general pattern of the magazines remains the same. They have constructed, and constantly reinforce, a state of 'femininity' through a continuing set of practices and beliefs. They are both specialist journals, produced for a single sex, and yet aim their contents at a general audience – every female is a potential reader who enjoys a particular aspect of a wide ranging number of female concerns. They remain as popular today as they were in the late 19th century, when they began to reach out to an expanding reading public.

Examples from both novels and firsthand accounts reinforce the apparent ease of women's participation in the war. They also draw on the experiences of both men and women at the battlefront and at home in England, trying to describe and express their thoughts and emotions after participating in a war that almost beggars description in its enormity of carnage and destruction. Examples from both literature and firsthand impressions will be included later in the book. However, at the end of both the First and Second World Wars, the majority of women returned to domesticity, appearing to re-accept their pre-war status as though little, if anything, had changed.

As well as a comparison between various magazines and examples of other literature, a small number of women have been interviewed. The interviews offer both a look at the domestic lives of these women and a glimpse into their involvement in war work, with some details of the dangers and hardships that they had to undergo.

These women are now mostly aged 90 years and over. Interviewing them must, naturally, take into consideration their memories, their assessment now of what they thought of the magazines then, and whether non-recognition could in part be due subconsciously to not wishing, as well as not being able, to remember. Seventy year-old memories may appear to be of little merit; time may have faded the details and confused the events. Their recollections of the magazines - an industry which is devoted to the production of future matter, the past being rarely seen as significant - must be influenced by personal selection, overlaid with nostalgia, with inevitable inaccuracies. Yet it is possible to pick up certain threads which are collectively repeated and suggest both the negative and positive influence of the magazines; and the memories themselves are of intrinsic value and historical interest.

For the historical and social background a number of books have been consulted. For corroboration of actual experience through fiction, certain novels and autobiographies have been drawn upon. A list of these is contained in the List of Works Consulted at the back of the book.

The intention is, therefore, to offer a reasonably balanced perspective - not the 'truth' about what really happened as memory and recollection play many tricks - but to attempt to point to the contradictions between what has been written in the magazines, what has been written in books based on actual experience and some of what has been remembered by a number of very elderly, but strong and courageous ladies with some extraordinary stories to tell.

CHAPTER I

The Changing Market – A Formula for Success:

"This magazine will aim at being to the girls a Counsellor, Playmate, Guardian, Instructor, Companion and Friend. It will help to train them in moral and domestic virtues, preparing them for the responsibilities of womanhood and for a heavenly home." (*The Girl's Own Paper*, 1880).

The Image

The first women's magazines were diaries and almanacs addressed mainly to women. Women's magazines, as we now recognise them, began in the second half of the 18th century. By the middle of the 19th century Samuel Beeton recognised the financial possibilities of a cheaper publication aimed at the middle classes, whose wives and daughters, no longer working alongside their menfolk, were increasingly involved in domestic duties in the home. Nineteenth century magazines were mainly concerned with manners and morals, personal appearance and the trivial routine of domestic duties. They reflected Victorian attitudes of male superiority, and the need to protect, indulge and shelter both middle and upper class women from the outside world.

The forerunners of today's mass-selling weeklies were launched at the beginning of the 20th century, with the growth of literacy, higher wages and new technology in printing and paper making. Magazines with informal and friendly titles were the first to provide practical information and advice on how to make a happy home for a lower middle class and working class readership. They reflected and reinforced the views of the average reader, and fitted their contents to suit the needs and interests they felt these views implied. Unlike those of earlier times, they were content to be trend followers rather than trend setters. They confined themselves almost entirely to domestic interests, paying little attention to the possibilities of widening their sphere of influence. Taking an active part in life outside the home was not presented as being a desirable extension of a woman's role.

The Great War's effect in broadening the lives of women stimulated new growth in magazine publication, helped by changing tastes as women's experience also changed. Yet, as will be seen, the new magazines continued to follow the pattern of those already in existence, paying little heed to the enormous changes in their readers' lives. Publishing policy seemed determined to continue 'the mixture as before', appearing to lag behind women's actual lives, except by re-angling their content with efforts to convince their readers of the need for 'Home Front' economies, and practical hints for sending comfort to an army which seemed so far away. The more sophisticated, government-backed propaganda campaigns were not established until just before the outbreak of the Second World War. Later chapters will examine the ongoing need for a comforting, familiar read, which the publishers continued to offer.

A number of new titles appeared on the market – though only a few came through the wartime upheavals in the publishing trade. By 1914, in conditions of war, their potential for influence through propaganda and editorial censorship added a new dimension to their importance as easily available and affordable literature. Yet the war itself is largely absent from the pages of the magazines of the period. In spite of the changes in society the magazines continued along the same lines of home-centred interests and attitudes. As long as they concentrated on the domestic sphere, continuing to promote a warm, friendly, supportive relationship with their readers, their success seemed to be assured.

In attempting to discover the breadth of influence of women's magazines and reasons for their continuing popularity, one needs to be aware of their general pattern. Women's magazines provide for the rhythms and routines of women's lives, in which private time for escape into a world of dreams and fantasies is precious, as work and leisure merge. Women's magazines draw on patterns which echo one another, offering knowledge, posing problems and providing solutions; each trying to capture its readers and make its particular familiarity a recurring part of their everyday world. The pattern of each magazine, however, has not appeared from nowhere; it is both the product of past developments and is constantly being reworked to reflect and keep pace with the changing experience of women's lives.

The specialism of women's magazines, which deliberately sets out to attract the attention of women only, is reinforced by various methods: the front covers and titles are used as advertisements for themselves, relating to women and the home - for example, *Woman and Home, Woman's Own, Ideal Home,* etc. By contrast, most men's magazines are aimed at particular groups of males, and cater for specific areas of a man's life - business, hobby or sporting interests. Their titles are deliberately aimed at the particular area they intend to cover: *Autocar, Photography, Computing,* etc. (Although there are now one or two more general magazines which follow a similar pattern to those in the women's market, such as *Arena* and *Gentleman's Quarterly.*) There is an implicit, shared assumption between editors, publishers and, it would seem, consumers, that women 'need' or 'want' to be instructed or kept up to date with the skills of femininity, whereas a more powerful and confident male already 'knows' all there is to know about being masculine, and can therefore enjoy pursuing a hobby or career without needing constantly to reiterate or reinforce his masculinity (though this has changed a little with the emphasis on the 'new man' of the 1980's and 1990's). On the whole, it is assumed that men do not need magazines to instruct them in the 'skills' of masculinity.

Women's magazines are, therefore, strongly concerned with promoting feminine 'values' and 'attitudes'. As Marjorie Ferguson, in *Forever Feminine,* suggests:

> "They tell women what to think and do about themselves, their lovers, their husbands, their parents, their children, their colleagues, neighbours and employers. The scope of their narrative direction is truly remarkable."

Added to this is the power of the advertising directed at women - the 'desirable, the possible and the purchasable'. The extent of acceptance of these messages and their influence can be multiplied many times through, for example, a mother's influence on her children, a wife's influence on her husband, and women's influence on one another.

The creation and maintenance of a 'cult of femininity' in women's magazines had become a basic function during the rapid expansion of their titles from the beginning of the 20th century. They played, and continue to play, a part in shaping the characteristics of femininity, because the picture of the world that they present is based on the assumption that each individual woman is a member of *her* society – the world of women. General issues are seen from the 'woman's angle' in contrast to most other repetitively produced literature, thus making the patterns of women's magazines a fascinating study. Events, attitudes, behaviour and products are thus, as Marjorie Ferguson says, given "reader relevance – the world viewed through a feminine lens". "What every woman knows" implies a common bond; a feeling of sharing and belonging between *all* women as members of every social group, and between the readers of a given magazine. The 'female' community remains the main component in the shared knowledge of homemaking, knitting, cooking, beauty hints, child care, and so on, and is reinforced in the narrative fiction which draws on romantic fantasies that have a common appeal. Women recognise what they already 'know' from daily experience.

Yet this 'common knowledge' is always selective and is based upon attitudes which may seem both natural and universal, but which are founded upon those prevailing within any period in society, and originating from the dominant male values and beliefs of what women want to read *within that society*. The continuing reinforcement of femininity, recognisable in the pages of women's magazines, underlines, specifically, the themes of domesticity and beauty; both rely to a large extent on the need to encourage the consumption of commodities, particularly because the magazines depend on advertisers for about 80% of their revenue. In spite of historical and social changes, the magazines continue to base their contents on this need.

Most of what is shared is based on familiar, re-created previous messages, though over a period of time re-angled, re-titled, re-adapted. Cleverly, the 'old' becomes the 'new'. Being 'good' at being a woman involves doing 'womanly' 'feminine' things at regular and appointed times. The rituals attached to making oneself beautiful and fashionable, to child-rearing, housework and cooking are presented as part of a continuous, symbolic process. In addition, women's magazines set agendas on which topics are important or permissible. The editors, backed by their publishers, by creating and fostering images and symbols of 'femininity' sustain both a readership and a market for their advertisers. They, in turn, respond to editors' perceptions of the female role – what women want and what will sell.

This image of a continuous, symbolic process throughout women's lives is not entirely at odds with reality, particularly in the emerging middle class homes of the early 20th century. Yet it does not stand alone. Throughout women's history, for the women of the working classes, the need to clean and keep house has existed *alongside* the necessity to work outside the home.

However, before a discussion of women's actual experience during the First World War can be fully detailed in contrast to the magazines, let us examine more closely the different areas within the magazines. It can thus be seen how the magazines changed their tone to fit the changes in society, attempting, at the same time, not to jeopardise the overall pattern of cosy domesticity and repetitive consumer need.

CHAPTER II

Change and Continuity – Manners, Morals and Fashion:

"Wartime's *your* time. Be sure you see to it."

Image and Reality

It is necessary to look more closely at the First World War magazines in order to see how much change there was in editorial policies: whether they accepted, adapted to or ignored what was happening around them. Examples have been taken from the following sections, and examined for the most readily revealed aspects of a) change and b) continuity. As far as possible women's actual experience will be incorporated, including looking at mobilisation, personal reactions to war, feelings about the pay and company at work, and the effects of war on women's health and moral lives. The sections will include:

Problem pages:- These used the most intimate tone of voice: prescriptive, didactic, ideal/typical of the multiple purposes of what journalists believe they and their products serve; entertaining at the same time as providing psychological and social support. They are based on a careful mixture of 'warmth, understanding and practical information', giving advice about sexual or familial anxieties, manners and morals, and 'worries' generally. However, they are necessarily a self-selecting, edited form of feedback. Arguably, this was, and still is, the page that attracted more readers than any other. Its popularity showed the pertinence of this kind of 'service' item for women, that of 'relationships' – women's relationship to men as potential or actual sexual partners, and their relationship to children.

Features:- These were editorial comments and articles, drawn from a wide range of considered interest: entertainment, life stories, 'real reader' dramas, case studies of emotional and sexual problems, general wisdom about coping with life. There was little inclusion of the reality of women's contribution to the war effort. There was continuity of ideas, with some incorporation of change. This format still retains similar principles – none of the women's magazines of the Gulf War period of 1991 offer features which contain references to the war, or women's contribution to it.

Fiction:- This drew, and still draws, upon aspiration and ambition, and escape through fantasy.

Both the changes themselves, and the difference between images of women, as depicted in the magazines, and their lives and experiences in reality, can be examined more easily by division into three eras: just pre-war, during the war and post-war. In the pre-war era the majority of women remained within the domestic environment, though a growing number of them found more freedom and independence through the suffragette movement, and better opportunities through education and work in shops and offices. By 1915 women were being directed into war work, and yet were still expected to cope with their work at home, or with everyday problems of living in lodgings or hostels. The post-war woman was, in the main, expected to return to her pre-war existence, giving up her job for the returning soldier, and picking up once again the reins of domesticity.

Let us now examine these changes in the three periods in far greater detail.

"WARTIME'S *YOUR* TIME. BE SURE YOU SEE TO IT"

The Handling of Change through the Problem Pages

The 'new woman' who appeared in the novels of the early 20th century – fighting for her independence, rallying for the vote, for a 'voice' in society – was mainly described through the eyes of men. Very few books were published offering a woman's point of view. This 'new woman' was often shown as being a problem for men to accept. Yet the women who were gradually emerging from their domestic roles and 'taking to the streets' through the suffragette movement, and working in factories, shops and offices from the early 1900s were, with the onset of war in 1914, suddenly thrust into an environment previously dominated by men. From being the target of criticism as the 'new' woman, they became a necessity as 'war-winning' women.

Throughout the period immediately before and until the end of the war the changes begun by women going out to work and wanting a fair deal were consolidated by the campaign for votes for women and the hardship of the war. Yet the Great War can be seen as the dividing line in the history of women's franchise. The trenches, rather than the drawing room, were finally responsible for the 'right to vote' for women and for their freedom from restricting clothes and conventions. 1914 brought change faster and more dramatically than anyone had imagined. The war had far more impact on women at home than granting the vote would have a few years later, and for a while the equilibrium between the sexes was thrown off its existing balance.

The replacement of male by female workers intensified the burning issue of 'dilution' – the substitution of unskilled and semiskilled for skilled workers. Confined to the duration of the war, the agreement laid down that in return for the acceptance of some dilution the employers would avoid any permanent restrictions of employment in favour of semi-skilled or female labour, and that at the end of the war, or before, the 'dilutees' would be the first to be dismissed. As Ann Oakley, in *Subject Women*, points out, this was a process which industry had been undergoing since the 1880s, but there was no doubt that some industrialists saw the war as an opportunity to strengthen their hand against the unions. Unskilled women workers took over men's jobs, and their consequent unpopularity with male workers was one thread in the antagonism the war bred between the sexes.

In *The Year 1914 Illustrated* a morale-boosting exercise offers a very carefully 'whitewashed' view of the dilution process. It states that "a certain dislocation of the labour market was anticipated as inevitable but, except in certain industries, the situation three months after the outbreak of war is not by any means as bad as was anticipated. The chief industries to suffer have been the cotton trade, the export of coal, and the manufacture and sales of articles recognised as luxuries". There is a positive attempt at optimism in the remark that "The recruiting of the New Army has relieved the labour market so far as males are concerned, but there are indications that the women's labour market is in a more serious condition. Here again the situation has been faced by the Government, a considerable sum of money having been allocated for helping forward industries crippled by the war."

The government initially decided to rely upon voluntary enlistment in fighting the war. However, when the new armies, in turn, suffered decimation in the battles of 1915 and 1916 it was found that Britain

31

had sacrificed an undue proportion of her best-trained and most courageous manhood. During 1915 the British Army in France suffered 300,000 casualties. In 1916, in a single day's battle which on lst July opened the Allied offensive on the Somme, it endured another 60,000 casualties, of whom one-third were killed. At Passchendaele, in 1917, the British advanced five miles at a cost of 400,000 men. Compulsory military service, first introduced early in 1916, could with advantage have come sooner; although the 'advantage', in hindsight, would have led only to more casualties at an earlier date. Between two and three million men were eventually recruited, first by voluntary enlistment, then by conscription.

As the war swallowed up great numbers of young men many women gained their first taste of independence. They were forced to come out from behind their lace curtains to take over shops or small businesses vacated by their husbands who had left for the Front, or to work in munitions, drive trucks, dig fields, drive buses, trams and trains and do many other jobs usually done by men, including work in banks and government departments.

In July 1914 there had been 212,000 women employed in what were to become the munitions industries. The figure for July 1915, 256,000, shows only a relatively small increase; but the great expansion of later 1915, combined with the impact of compulsory military service in early 1916, is seen in the next July figure, 520,000, an increase of over 100 per cent. In the last year of the war there was a further increase of well over 100,000. In industry as a whole the total employment of women and girls over ten years of age between 1914 and 1918 increased by about 800,000, from 2,179,000 to 2,971,000. By February 1917 the total number of, for example, bus conductresses leapt from the timorous handful of the previous year to about 2,500, some half of whom, apparently, were former domestic servants.

Over the whole war it is transport which shows the biggest proportionate increase in women's employment – from 18,000 in 1914 to 117,000 in 1918. And it is domestic service which is the one industry that showed a decline; from 1,658,000 in 1914 to 1,258,000 in 1918.

How did the Problem Pages Handle this Change in Women's Roles?

In one sense women's magazines were responsible for romanticising matrimony. It was presented as the pinnacle of every woman's happiness and the goal of every girl's ambition. Most serials ended at the altar, and home was considered all important. Yet the War rudely interrupted the neat lives of countless couples whose future – a few years of engagement, then marriage and children – was changed with the arrival of call-up papers:-

> "My first boyfriend wanted to get married before going to the Front. I wanted to wait. Then he wanted to get married at Christmas, while on leave. I refused... then he got killed."

This was Margaret, interviewed at the age of 98. Married twice after the loss of her first fiancé, her life has contained much further suffering, as will be shown later in Chapter IX. Elizabeth, interviewed at the age of 99, also lost her fiancé during the First World War. She never married, and still finds the memory of her loss extremely painful.

It is possible to see the wartime concern with the continuation of the status quo in changing circumstances and conflicting needs. In an effort not to let standards slide advisers in the magazines drew the line at waiting to meet a man in the street or accepting a typewritten proposal of marriage, but expressed admiration for a correspondent who felt that she should offer to pay her share of their outings as her fiancé had not much money. Another agony aunt, quoted in Robin Kent's *Aunt Agony Advises*, advised a young reader to think carefully before leaving a comfortable home and trying to live on the meagre separation allowance provided for wives of serving men. This rose to some extent between 1914 and 1917; but the basic rate for a non-commissioned soldier was 12s 6d per week. The rate for a sergeant major was 23s 0d per week. The rate for each child under fourteen was 3s 0d per week. However, in a change of concern which reflected wartime propaganda, the 'auntie' continued:-

"I don't want to influence you against your mother's wishes, but if it were my own case, I would rather have him go away as my husband. For one reason, if he came back wounded, no one could dispute your right to nurse him."

In Terry Jordan's *Agony Columns*, ending an engagement was seen as a great and noble sacrifice:-

"Dear 'Faith', it looks as if your soldier boy is a very extra sort of hero, doesn't it? Isn't it probable that he feels that he cannot bind you to your engagement now that he is a cripple for life? His letter is surely not the result of a sudden ceasing of his love for you, but rather the outcome of great and noble self-sacrifice... Write to him again, and ask him straightforwardly whether his incapacity is the only thing which comes between him and you, and then, if you truly love him, as I believe you do, reassure him that you would marry him under any circumstances..."

From our present point of view, these two quotes suggest a very strongly worded need to reinforce the 'rights' and 'privileges' of the woman's role. These rights did not, however, extend to those women in professions such as teaching or nursing, etc., who wished to get married but knew that this meant an end to their careers. Dorothy Moriarty (now aged 102) in *Dorothy, The Memoirs of a Nurse* pointed out that so much was frowned on and forbidden in those days: smoking, socialising with the housemen, marriage. If a nurse dared to marry while she was training, that was the end of her career. She goes on to point out, however, that in those days of wartime marriages there were nurses who would risk their final certificates. "We would conspire together to keep her secret. Harder to hide was a case of morning sickness, but somehow we managed that too!"

Despite the onset of war and the meteoric rise in the numbers of war widows, a conscious decision appears to have been taken by the magazines to publish very few of their letters. This absence may have reflected a decision, for reasons of morale, that these letters should be answered privately. Robin Kent (in *Aunt Agony Advises*) noted: "Death stalked the problem page only by implication." Information was given on how to claim a widow's pension, and on how to contact the War Office to find out why letters from the Front had ceased. Women were given advice on self-sufficiency and how to manage their financial affairs. In 1916-1917 the widow of an officer who had died under the age of thirty-five received £36 0s per annum. If he was over thirty-five the widow received £42 0s. If he was over forty-five the widow received £48 0s per annum. For a non-commissioned soldier the rates were £10 0s, £12 6s and £15 0s respectively. The first child of the widow received 5s 0d weekly; the second 3s 6d, the third and subsequent children 2s 0d each per week. Orphans received 5s 0d each per week.

The number of men killed in the war enormously increased the 'surplus' women, so that very nearly one woman in every three had to be self-supporting; innumerable homes had been broken up and there had been brought into existence a great class of 'new poor'. Prices were nearly double what they had been in 1914, and the women who had been able to live upon their small allowances or fixed incomes could do so no longer. Yet the need and opportunity for more jobs for women did not immediately lead the magazines to an acceptance of work as an alternative to marriage.

Despite the implications for women of the loss of so many future partners, their future prospects were still seen in traditional terms. Again, in *Aunt Agony Advises:-*

> "We are all training for professions and mean to be happy and prosperous in our careers if possible, but we one and all realise that marriage is the vocation of healthy sensible girls and we are not going to pass by love for any high-flown notions about careers and fame..."

By 1919, however, the problem pages found themselves dealing with a rash of letters from women trying to cope with the aftermath of war (Robin Kent again):-

> "Some girls found that they could not bear the sight of their returning hero. But if one girl ditched a crippled, demobbed soldier there were still 'a great many girls who want to marry him' – even a cripple had a value in a market denuded of young men."

Readers whose men had been killed were encouraged to mourn for a socially acceptable period (see page 43 for details), and then to think about the future. Again, in *Aunt Agony Advises*, a reader was told by *Peg's Paper* in June 1919 that "It is no use living in the past, my dear, and what might have been." Her new man would fill her life as completely as the other had done, and "I am sure your first boy would wish you to be happy, for life without love is very lonely for a girl."

By November 1918 the first inter-racial marital problems arose, with soldiers from all areas of the British Empire, including Canadian, Australian, New Zealand and Indian troops, meeting English girls for the first time. This new area of concern was raised, for example, in *The Family Herald* of November 1918. (Quoted in *Aunt Agony Advises*.) Interestingly, only the answer to the question was given thus:-

> "You are acting wisely in using your influence to prevent marriage between two people of widely different racial types, so long as you act and speak with great discretion. Interference in questions of marriage often has the effect of hurrying unwise youth into the very mistake that is feared. But it is your duty, placed as you are, to point out, of course, with delicacy and affection, that all the difficulties inherent in marriage are trebled in the case of men and women of different races binding themselves together."

However, more liberal attitudes to acceptability in marriage seemed gradually to emerge by the 1920s.

Although four years of misery, death and shortages led girls in the Twenties to dream of gaiety, laughter and happiness, the new spinster who 'charlestoned', smoked, shingled her hair and wore lipstick, was now faced with strong competition in her search for a husband. The bravado of tone shown in the magazines with regard to there being less necessity to rush into marriage had, however, a hollow ring, as Robin Kent points out:-

> "Your modern maiden is not nonplussed if, at the ripe age of thirty-five or over, she finds herself husbandless. She is possessed of courage and a reckless independence

which enables her to stand alone and fight her own battle, and she doesn't feel embittered if the right man dawdles instead of hastening to be on the step to realise her worth."

Lynn Macdonald, in *The Roses of No Man's Land*, notes that many of those who did not marry turned into a generation of redoubtable maiden aunts – because most of the men of their age-group whom they might have married never came back from the war, and those women who had served in their capacity of ambulance drivers, nurses or VADs (Voluntary Aid Detachments) came back to a changed world. Of course, some did marry, but the others were not content to return to their old life of busy idleness, even if circumstances had made it possible. Nor were they content to sit around mourning their lot as the 'surplus women' which society unflatteringly called them in the twenties and thirties. Having proved beyond argument during the war that women could do anything, they set out to carve themselves a place in what was still a man's world. They moved wholesale into commerce. They became teachers, doctors, social workers, pharmacists, journalists, ran dairies and chicken farms. They won the vote and the right to work in the face of formidable opposition and the continuing philosophy that a woman's place was in the home, even though such hopes as many marriageable girls had had of husband and children lay buried with their men on some far-off battlefield.

Certainly, changes in relations between the sexes did not seem to result in new freedom for many of the girls who worked in the munitions factories. Margaret stated:

"I did not notice women giving up their jobs. Majority got married after the war. The factory girls got married in a church next to the tram depot which was dedicated to soldiers and factory girls."

Changes in Manners and Etiquette

The war brought sudden changes in manners and etiquette, from the decision as to which perfume to co-ordinate with which dress, in *The Ladies Field* of June 1914, to the same magazine in October 1914, when the magazine felt it was self-indulgent to buy luxuries.

There were many other sweeping social changes. The slackening of the duties of a chaperone allowed young people to spend time with each other during soldiers' leave, though in *Tit Bits* this in itself raised another problem:-

> "His mother (Cheltenham) asks the curious question, 'Which should a soldier home for a few days' leave visit first – his fiancée or his mother?' This is a delicate matter to decide. Personally, we should say he owes his first duty to his mother. But the best way out of the difficulty would be for the mother to invite the fiancée to spend the period of leave as her guest."

By 1916 parents who demanded descriptions of events at the Front from those home on leave were described by *Betty's Weekly* as showing a 'want of thought', and young people suffering this situation were told to confront their parents and 'not to make martyrs of yourself as you are doing'.

Discussion of events at the Front did not seem to be part of war etiquette. When interviewed, Joan said:-

> "Three of my brothers were in the war. One was wounded – he did not want to talk about it."

Jane confirmed this in her interview:-

> "All my brothers fought. One brother was blinded in the war. Never talked about it."

Although many of those who served kept diaries, and sent letters (which were heavily censored) home, discussion of the war when the men were on leave or had completed their service does not appear to have taken place.

Prior to the war, among the working class, women had worked as hard as men but for far less remuneration. Hard industrial work had been a commonplace in the lives of very many women since before the Industrial Revolution. They were the industrial drudges of the community, earning an average wage of 11s 7d per week, about one third of the male average. They worked as domestic servants, cleaners and dressmakers, milliners, governesses, in the cotton mills, in shops and hotels and in luxury goods manufacture. Ethel worked in domestic service before the war:-

"There was no hot water, no Hoovers. Just a long brush for the carpets. I had to carry coal up four or five flights of stairs, scrub steel fenders with an emery board. We needed a sack of coal for each fire. I was on board wages – we had to buy our own food out of 12s 6d per week. We had to have three uniform dresses, six yards each, of print material. I had to make them myself. I had no spare time for reading – could not afford magazines on the money I was left with – 3s 4d per week.

I used to go to Selfridges on my afternoon off and stand at the perfume counter. A little bottle of Californian Poppy cost 2s 6d! I could not afford that.

When the young men in the house enlisted, it was too hard for us (the female servants) to fill the coal scuttles. I went to work at Woolwich Arsenal."

Doris worked on a farm, and then went into domestic service:-

"I went into service in the big houses. There were six or seven maids for one family. It was hard, with no electrical help. There was nothing else for a girl to do. I did all right – went from one house to another for more money. But the wages were very poor, and the hours very long. I remember having to queue for food – we struggled in those days. You were either rich or poor, nothing in between. I was given material for two print dresses each Christmas in service. I had to supply my own uniform. We had very poor wages – 2s per week to start with. Caps and aprons had to come out of your own money. I started work at 7 a.m., with breakfast for the master, until eight at night. Scrubbing, cleaning, polishing. We had no time to read magazines while in service, we had no leisure. I went to see my mother on my day off. We had every other Sunday off after washing the dinner dishes and getting tea ready.

On the other Sunday we had to go to church. No night off, for fear you had a baby. No idea what babies were!"

As shown on page 41 the first effects of the war were disastrous for the women in the 'sweated' and dressmaking trades. Before the end of 1915, however, the first attempts at 'dilution' in munitions and ordnance factories brought an expansion and change in the work done by female factory workers. While for some only a very slight change in job was involved, there were other cases where large numbers of girls and women were drawn in who had never previously worked in a factory or workshop.

Whether there was a rise in spending on consumer goods, including magazines and the products advertised in them, as a result of the increased earning power of the 'wartime' woman, is an interesting speculation. *Betty's Weekly* was aimed at working girls, and reflected the dramatic changes of readers' lives after the exodus of their men to the Front. A girl working in an armament factory could earn considerably more than a 'tommy' in the ranks. By the last year of the war, the female munitions workers were earning well over £2 per week, and other women factory workers could count on about 25s a week. This dramatically changed the traditional manners of courting couples, as shown in *Aunt Agony Advises*:-

> "I'm making a good screw, 30 shillings a week, and my boy, who is in the Welsh Fusiliers hasn't much more than that in pennies. So being the one who has the most money, I, in the meanwhile, want to pay for our seats when we go to the pictures, but he won't let me.
> "The boys are making so little money at the present, so why shouldn't every one of their sweethearts do the entertaining for a bit..."

The changes in social life for many young women were more dramatic, and those at work away from home had to get used to life in hostels or lodgings. Ethel lived in lodgings while she was working at Woolwich Arsenal:-

"I lived in lodgings in Plumstead. I had a long journey – I left the factory after 7 p.m. and got home after eight. One of my landladies only gave me a herring for my supper when I got home."

Changes in Fashion

A patriotic fervour to help the war effort by cutting down on luxury items such as clothing, or household goods, led to large-scale unemployment, particularly in the cotton trade, by the end of 1914. Yet in the interim before the War Office was sufficiently organised to redeploy the men and women who had been employed in this industry, the magazines encouraged a less enthusiastic campaign of reduction in spending on fashion. Both shortage of materials and shortage of labour, together with the desire to help with the war effort, however, led to permanent fashion changes which were part of a revolution in the feminine image. Terry Jordan, in *Aunt Agony Advises*, makes this point:-

> "When gently nurtured middle class girls rolled up their once full sleeves and poured out tea for soldiers at Victoria Station, or nursed wounded men in emergency hospitals, they sloughed off their elaborate costumes permanently."

The materials became plainer as people talked about economising. For working girls skirts went up, stays went out. The pre-war layered look of tunic over underskirt was adapted by replacing the underskirt with breeches or doing without it altogether. Trailing skirts were impossible in many jobs. Chauffeuring or bus conducting required agility which was difficult in a long dress, and woman landworkers wore breeches. Women enjoyed the somewhat military appearance of the new fashion and the sense that, for the first time, class distinction was not immediately discernible from the clothes they wore. Many of them had enough money in their wage packets to be able to follow fashion for the first time. The changes in fashion from 1818 to 1918 were quite dramatic.
Yet the changes were very slow to filter through into the magazines. The pre-war fashions in *Woman's Life*, 1914, showed women wearing hats, long hobble skirts, gloves, etc. *Home Chat* during the war, in

EXHIBITION
of WAR ECONOMY DRESS.
MUST · BE · SEEN · BY · EVERYONE
Grafton Galleries. Bond Street.
10 to 6. From 3rd to 31st August (Inclusive)

The National Standard Dress will be demonstrated by
Mrs Allan Hawkey. The Inventor,
who will Lecture Daily.

MANY OTHER ATTRACTIONS
Orchestra will play daily.
Admission 1/3d Inclusive of Tax.

1915, still showed the same or similar fashions in the drawings which appeared in the features and stories, but the fashion section showed skirts as being ankle length, and looser fitting. Patriotism did filter through into the fashion section, as *Home Chat*, 1915, suggests:-

"Wear white this summer, and you'll be helping the manufacturer to keep going till our English chemists have discovered how to make coloured dyes to take the place of those we have been getting from Germany."

My Weekly of 1916, also showed very little change. By 1918, *Woman's Life* was showing fashions in the new 'Victory' colour, though the skirts were still long. The 'Victory' colour was given as 'Foch' blue – "clear blue and rich in effect, and combines beautifully with black". In 1919 *Home Chat* still advocated that there was 'nothing much that is fresh to tell about tailor-made skirts'. In *Vogue* of 1916, however, the fashions were as elaborate as they had been prior to the war, both in use of materials and in style, in spite of recommending 'smart fashions for limited incomes':-

"A most becoming tea gown is sketched at the lower right of this page. It is of rose silk with a tight pointed bodice and a full straight skirt, finished at the hem with a pleated ruffle. Over this is worn a trailing coat of deeper rose chiffon with kimono sleeves. The front is finished with silver braid and silver tassels, and a great full-blown rose."

The war also "drove the first nail into the coffin of elaborate mourning", as Robin Kent, in *Aunt Agony Advises*, remarked. Shortage of material, emphasis on economy and, for the first time in any war, the extent of the carnage, prevented mourners from assuming a distinctive status. Furthermore, as Grace, one of the interviewees, pointed out:-

"Mourning was for a year, some families more than others, if you could afford it. Many gone during the war. Black bands were worn instead – saved your face that way."
Had the period of mourning remained as specified by *The Queen* at the beginning of the 20th century – "The strict period is twelve

A most becoming tea gown is sketched at the lower right on this page. It is of rose silk with a tight pointed bodice and a full straight skirt, finished at the hem with a pleated ruffle. Over this is worn a trailing coat of deeper rose chiffon with kimono sleeves. The front is finished with silver braid and silver tassels, and a great full-blown rose.

(*Right*) *If a tea gown has a tight bodice and a full skirt of rose-coloured silk beneath a trailing coat of deeper rose-coloured chiffon bound with silver braid—well, then it just can't help being becoming*

months; ten months black and two and a half months half mourning" –
there would, by November 1918, have been scarcely a single
colourfully dressed woman left.

As early as 1916 this letter appeared (shown in *Aunt Agony
Advises*):-

> "The usual period of mourning would be a month. Only
> a very little quiet visiting is done amongst intimate friends
> during that time... Nowadays mourning is greatly shortened
> and even, in some cases, not worn at all."

Woman's Life September 1916 agreed with this:-

> "The latest custom in widows' mourning is to wear
> crape as a trimming only, and to leave this off after six or
> eight months. Some widows, however, do not wear it at
> all."

These letters were examples of a significant change in the
previously strict adherence to mourning etiquette; only seven months
earlier a previous letter had shown the misunderstanding of a decision
to forgo mourning by a young woman's friends and her late lover's
relations (again, in *Aunt Agony Advises*):-

> "I have lost my dear, brave soldier boy and all my
> friends are angry with me because I do not wear black. But
> neither he nor I approved of mourning; he always begged
> me never to put it on for him, and so I do not... it is so hard
> to be looked upon as heartless that I have nearly given way
> more than once. Do you think I ought to do so?"

The answer given was:-

> "No, my dear, I do not. You are showing as much
> respect to his memory by doing as he preferred and as you
> promised, as by wearing the deepest symbols of woe."

Changes in Religion

Conventional religious attitudes also changed during the First World War. Prayers for the safety of loved ones did not seem adequate, and a fashion for the occult became a widely used alternative – following an historical precedent in times of crisis. This trend was picked up in the magazines: an engaged woman, for example, encouraged not to lose hope, despite having received no news, was reassured in Leech's *Lady Companion*:-

> "Do not give up hope; you will hear from your fiancé soon, but he has not been able to write because he has been dangerously ill. He will recover, and will get leave in about a month's time."

A reader in *Tit Bits* 1916, wrote:-

> "Miss C: Two years ago, a palmist told me that I should be married in my twenty-third year... I was within a week of my twenty-third birthday, and no man had ever shown any sign of wishing to make me his wife. I had quite abandoned all hope of the prophecy coming true, when in the very last week of the year I chanced to meet a young officer home on short leave from the Front... The next day he proposed... and the following day I was a bride. The palmist's credit was saved..."

Examples like these were probably forerunners of the growing and now well-established horoscopes which are still widely published in today's magazines.

The aftermath of war left many previously religious people finding it hard to reconcile their faith with the horrors of war, as well as the disappointments and difficulties of a future without the support and help of a man. The problem pages of the magazines in the 1920s began to show a quiet but distinct revolution in society's attitude to religion. Previously, religious convictions had been openly expressed and reinforced by those with social and legal authority. By the 1920s religion had become a matter of private conscience (as quoted in *Aunt Agony Advises*):-

"An ordinary citizen of the rank and file is not justified in offering gratuitous and unsolicited criticisms on the conduct of his or her fellow citizens, unless there is distinct wrongdoing which threatens injury to others."

The image of femininity shown in books and magazines, even during the war, appeared to be paramount; a woman was still seen and depicted as the 'Angel of the Hearth' and the maker of the home, and expected to fulfil this role without question. Family life was posited as their sole existence. Middle class women knew little of the world of industry, and did not expect to work. Although there were a few jobs available for single middle class women before the war, such as teaching, nursing, secretarial work, as governesses and nannies, it was still rare for a married middle class woman to have a job. If their husbands' earnings dropped they had to suffer genteel poverty, for there were few opportunities for them to earn extra money. The world of employment before 1914 was dominated by men, while women's work was often invisible or classed as unimportant. Domestic work was simply seen as women's duty. They were not encouraged to be ambitious, nor to want anything other than a comfortable home, complete with husband and children to look after.

In the next chapter it will be seen how the magazine image compares with the reality.

CHAPTER III

Women at Work:

"It is simply splendid to see how readily our nation has responded to the call of her country... Everybody is busy and, best of all, everybody is working with a whole-hearted willingness."

In 1914, with the outbreak of war, attitudes towards femininity changed very rapidly in reality. The war turned the idea of woman's place on its head. While the men went to the Front women replaced them in jobs that would never have been thought suitable or possible before. As has been previously shown, women became stokers, foundry workers, bus drivers, machine gun manufacturers, etc. Here are some of the jobs taken on by the women who were interviewed: -

Mary: "I started working in the Rowntree factory in 1915, when I was fourteen. They were making blocks of plain chocolate for the troops. I worked in the packing room, putting the seals on the top and bottom of the boxes. I can see the trays now. After the war I stayed there until I got married."

Jane: "I was twenty-one in 1914 when the war broke out. I was working at J. Lyons tea shop at 215 Oxford Street, London. We were directed into war work. I went to the Aircraft Manufacturing Co. at Colindale, Hendon, where we were put to work in the upholstery department, at first stuffing large cushions with horsehair for Swift's flying boats. We worked long hours and overtime. I had to get a workman's ticket to Colindale for 3d. The horsehair was clean but not too good to look at! After this we did doors and cushions for De Havilland aircraft. I remember Miss Margaret Bonfield coming to Hendon with her banners, 'Women of the world unite', to form the first union for better wages –

ABOVE Women road sweepers
working in the Borough of
Ealing in London
LEFT Post woman collecting
mail from a pillar box

which were then 13s a week and extra for overtime."

"I remember King George and Queen Mary with Princess Mary coming to visit the factory in 1916. Mr G. De Havilland and his co-designer used a mock-up of a plane's engine in front of our benches to test a missile firing through the centre of the propeller."

"I then went to work at Schweppes factory, where we sent out thousands of nuts and screws to factories for aircraft. I went to High Wycombe in 1918 and worked in a furniture factory making trench rattles for gas attacks."

Margaret: "I worked at Woolwich Arsenal all through the war, in the Royal Army Ordnance Department. I was directed there. I spent most of the war loading shells on to railway trucks, and packing them. I was living in a hostel, and did both day and night work. At night, we were so tired we used to lie on the ammunition – it could have blown us all up!"

"The things I used to do – mad! Got on a tram one morning to go to work. Went up to the front and said, 'I can drive this.' 'Come on then'. He let me drive all the way to Abbey Wood!"

Millie: "I worked at Rowntree, making fancy boxes. I had plenty of friends there. I always worked. I never married, looked after my mother."

Victoria: "I was twenty-four at the beginning of the war. My sister and I ran a professional women's club. They were a nice lot of educated women. I worked at weekends in the munitions factory with my sister in Battersea. We took over on Sundays to let those working during the week have a rest."

BLACK CAT CIGARETTES

INSTRUCTING RECRUITS
AS TO USE OF TRAVELLING FIELD KITCHEN.

BLACK CAT CIGARETTES

BUS CONDUCTOR.

BLACK CAT CIGARETTES

CLEANING A LOCOMOTIVE.

BLACK CAT CIGARETTES

STEAM ROLLER DRIVER.

BLACK CAT CIGARETTES

GLASS MANUFACTURE.

BLACK CAT CIGARETTES

FLOUR MILL.

BLACK CAT CIGARETTES

V.A.D. WOMAN.

WOMEN ON WAR WORK

No. 3. Instructing Recruits as to use of Field Travelling Kitchen.

IN civil life very few men know much about cooking or how to manage a stove. As many men cooks are required for field kitchens, capable women are employed to instruct them in the use of field kitchens, and in simple cookery.

Issued by
CARRERAS LIMITED
ESTAB. 1788
LONDON & MONTREAL
ENG. QUE.

WOMEN ON WAR WORK

No. 41. BUS CONDUCTOR.

VERY smart and workmanlike are these girls, and on the whole they are very good-natured in spite of all the difficulties and trials such work brings. Their work is fatiguing, their hours are long, but they are "doing their bit" in this very useful way.

Issued by
CARRERAS LIMITED
ESTAB. 1788
LONDON & MONTREAL
ENG. QUE.

WOMEN ON WAR WORK

No. 48. CLEANING A LOCOMOTIVE.

THE great engines which draw the trains on our railways must be kept clean or they will soon become useless. Formerly, this was work done entirely by men, but it has been proved that women are very capable and thorough, where they have been given such work to do.

Issued by
CARRERAS LIMITED
ESTAB. 1788
LONDON & MONTREAL
ENG. QUE.

WOMEN ON WAR WORK

No. 39. STEAM ROLLER DRIVER.

EVEN in this heavy work, women have done wonderfully well, showing both nerve and tenacity which has surprised a good many people. Still, it is one of the war time occupations which they will no doubt be glad to relinquish when they are no longer needed.

Issued by
CARRERAS LIMITED
ESTAB. 1788
LONDON & MONTREAL
ENG. QUE.

WOMEN ON WAR WORK

No. 38. GLASS MANUFACTURE.

ALTHOUGH women have shewn that they can very efficiently fill men's places in peace, as in other kinds of industry, they will probably be very glad to leave it to the men, when the latter come back again.

Issued by
CARRERAS LIMITED
ESTAB. 1788
LONDON & MONTREAL
ENG. QUE.

WOMEN ON WAR WORK

No. 5. FLOUR MILL.

SOME of the work in a flour mill requires a good deal of muscular strength, and in peace days such work was considered unsuitable for women. However, when far spent came the women proved themselves quite equal to the strenuous tasks required of them.

Issued by
CARRERAS LIMITED
ESTAB. 1788
LONDON & MONTREAL
ENG. QUE.

WOMEN ON WAR WORK

No. 43. V.A.D. WOMAN.

EVERYONE knows the smart uniform of the Women's Voluntary Aid Detachment. These women have cheerfully undertaken, as volunteers, all kinds of duties; and they have done all of them thoroughly well.

Issued by
CARRERAS LIMITED
ESTAB. 1788
LONDON & MONTREAL
ENG. QUE.

ABOVE Woman tram driver a
Lowestoft; there was much
resistance from the men and
by the end of the War there
was still only a handful of
women drivers

Donated by Jane Waller and Michael Vaughan Rees

Pride in their work comes through very strongly in the testimonies of many of the women interviewed, and so does the sense of freedom many felt when comparing their war work with the confines of home or a typical women's job:-

Sybil: "I was a student and teacher at seventeen during the war. I scrubbed floors in King's Hospital, while still at school. I took a barrow and collected old iron for recycling; and collected stamps, envelopes and note paper – to write letters for soldiers in hospital or to give them to write themselves."

Yet Radclyffe Hall, in *The Well of Loneliness*, points out that the pride of helping in the war effort was overlaid with concern about having to return to their former lives at the end of the war:-

"... a mighty event had slipped into the past, had gone from them into the realms of history; something terrible yet splendid, a oneness with life in its titanic struggle against death. Not a woman of them all but felt vaguely regretful in spite of the infinite blessing of peace, for no one could know what the future might hold of trivial days filled with trivial actions."

The war put conventional views about sexual roles under strain. Yet at the same time that they were working as long hours as men, learning new jobs and earning better wages than had previously been thought possible, women's ideas about work were as fixed as men's. They felt they had no right to take a job from a man with a family to support, and that the changes in their lives were merely part of the different world of war. Rose, a retired teacher, felt very strongly about this:-

"I did not believe in equal pay at the time, and would not join the teachers' union. I felt they were very 'anti-men'. The men had families to support, and needed more money. I do agree with equal pay now – a lot of women have just as many calls on their money!"

While men had to think again about what women could, or could not, do at work, it did not alter their belief that women alone were responsible for the home life of the nation.

During the first few months of the war unemployment rose rapidly, as a sudden patriotic desire arose to economise, cutting back on domestic servants or workers in the luxury goods trade. Men rushed to enlist. Many people tried to play a part in the war effort. Middle class and wealthy women took up voluntary work, and started to knit or sew for the troops. They knitted socks, waistcoats, helmets, comforters, mittens, body belts. They knitted at the theatre, in trains and trams, in parks and parlours, in the intervals of eating in restaurants, of serving in canteens. Certainly some of the women interviewed were determined to 'do their bit':-

Grace: "I knitted mittens, knee caps, balaclavas, and gloves for the soldiers. I sent parcels to the Front. I had a brother in the Civil Service who went into the catering corps during the war. He begged for a marrow bone to make soup – I sent one in a parcel, with some faggots – the parcel fell to bits when it was opened! I wrote letters, filled with anything I could think of to make them longer."

Dolly: "I knitted socks. I remember wanting to help the war effort, so I answered an advertisement in the paper for knitting. When the wool arrived, it was a very large bundle of oiled wool. I still remember the greasy feeling. No one would help me with it!"

Here is a rather biased view of this effort from *1914 Illustrated*:-

"*Relief Funds*:- On the outbreak of war the Prince of Wales inaugurated a National Fund for the relief of distress at home. His appeal was generously responded to by all classes, and at the end of October the fund totalled upwards of £3,500,000.

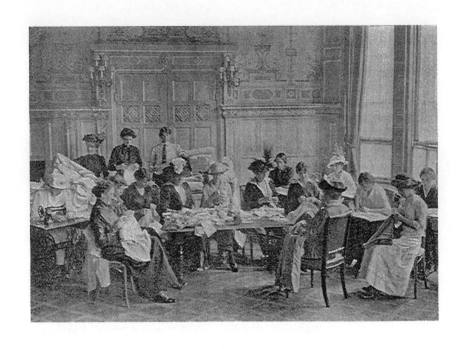

Funds were also raised for medical supplies and ambulances for the wounded soldiers. A further call was made when the Belgian refugees flocked over to this country for protection from the enemy. Hospitality was provided in all parts of the country for these friendly aliens, some being entertained in private houses and others at public buildings, like the Alexandra Palace."

Many middle class women found their lives in turmoil. Factory and munitions work lured their servants away. The pay was better, the hours shorter, and their free time was their own. Many who were abandoned by their staff had to move to more manageable homes. At the same time, many working class women had no other jobs to turn to, for the government at this stage, early in the war, did not consider the idea of using women to do men's jobs in industry. Indeed, at this time, most government and military men thought that women should 'stay out of the way' while men fought; the limit of support was, as seen above, supposed to be knitting for the troops or nursing. This was endorsed in, for example, *Home Chat* July 1915:-

"Half the people who want to help and don't know how to, could grow SOMETHING TO EAT – pigs or rabbits, or potatoes, or goats, or beans – if only they would... Growing the finest sweet peas that ever were grown will do nothing to win the war."

However, times began to change rapidly; as more men enlisted, many businesses became short staffed. Government contracts for uniforms etc., led to an increase in factory work. Women became increasingly visible in the city streets. Early 1915 was the turning point for women's employment, as they went into the production of munitions and were placed in industries on work customarily done by men; though they were accepted with great reluctance into most of the skilled trades, as has been shown on page 31.

For many civilians the war did not bring immediate or dramatic change. Joan recalled certain wartime incidents, but her way of life was not affected a great deal:-

WOMEN'S
GREAT PATRIOTIC PROCESSION

TO BE FOLLOWED

BY A DEPUTATION TO MR. LLOYD GEORGE,

TO DEMAND

THE RIGHT TO SERVE

OUR COUNTRY AND HELP TO WIN THE WAR.

Women, by their labour, can support the men in the trenches, who are saving the country from the fate that has befallen Gallant Belgium.

EVERY WOMAN SHOULD JOIN THE PROCESSION WHICH TAKES PLACE

On SATURDAY, JULY 17th.

FORM UP ON THE VICTORIA EMBANKMENT AT 2.30 p.m. START AT 3.30 p.m.

SEND IN YOUR NAMES TO LINCOLN'S INN HOUSE, KINGSWAY, W.C.

"We have a great unused force, the force of women, and when it is organised we will show the Germans what we as the British people can do."

MRS. PANKHURST at the London Pavilion, July 1st.

CHARLES JONES & Co., LTD., Printers, 27-29, Cursitor Street, E.C.

"We lived in a village. There were eight of us in the family at the beginning of the war. Each village had its own searchlight. The German Zeppelins used to come over. We lived beside a church with a very high steeple, so we used to sleep in a cottage by the river in case the church was bombed. We were a farming family, so we had no food shortages. One of my brothers worked on the land, and therefore did not have to go to war. The other mothers in the village were very bitter about this, so he used to go out the back door to the fields. It was quiet, and life did not change during the war."

Mary, too, had a quiet life during the war:-

"We lived in a small village. There were four children. It was quiet during the war, with no bombing. We were not really desperate for food. I did not do anything for the war effort."

Many middle class girls' horizons actually narrowed. Vera Brittain was very aware of this:-

....as the War continued to wear out strength and spirits, the middle-aged generation, having irrevocably yielded up its sons, began to lean with increasing weight upon its daughters. Thus the desperate choice between incompatible claims - by which the women of my generation, with their carefully trained consciences, have always been tormented - showed signs of afflicting us."

The men left for the Front, and they remained at home with their parents, although many did what they could to help:-

Rose: "Many middle class women helped in hospitals. Groups of girls went to see wounded soldiers in local hospitals - although I did not go. I worked in the Casualty Office."

Molly: "I knitted balaclavas and scarves. We adopted soldiers, and sent parcels (hard-boiled eggs, chocolate and tobacco)."

Betty: "I worked in an office part-time, for War Pensions, assisting soldiers when discharged or invalided out – giving information and interviewing them."

Many working class girls merely changed one factory job for another, or took on jobs that the men had been doing and, as we have seen, found themselves working harder and for longer hours than before.

The wartime workers were not an homogeneous group. The majority were young and working class, but there were significant numbers of older married women and middle class volunteers. There were bound to be tensions as women from such different backgrounds came together in the factory. Groups of friends assembled according to the work they were in – the light gun factory, the shell shops, the clerical workers and the canteen helpers – and these groups seemed to keep together. Many women were labouring under exceptional strain in munitions factories, shipyards and transport.

Life outside the factory, too, had its problems – food or housing shortages and long hours of travelling, on top of the normal burdens of housekeeping, made life even harder for working class women. Grace remembers the difficulty in getting food:-

"I remember getting up at five in the morning to queue up for a loaf of bread – and then it was mouldy."

The Times of 10th December 1917 reported the foods that were in short supply. A week later, it reported: 'The food queues continue to grow'. Outside the dairy shops of certain multiple firms in some parts of London women began to line up for margarine as early as five o'clock on Saturday morning, some with infants in their arms, and others with children at their skirts.

Added to this was the anxiety about relatives and friends who had joined the forces.

Lack of child care arrangements could stop a woman from working outside the home, no matter how much she needed the money:-

> "In the First World War I couldn't go out to work, because I had a baby of two and a half... I could have got a job at the Arsenal, but I would have had to do night work. I wanted my mother to look after my baby so I could go out to work, but she refused." (Extract from *Out of the Cage* by Gail Braybon and Penny Summerfield)

She took the classical women's option: bought a sewing machine and made clothes at home for Woolwich workers.

In the working environment concern about office propriety was quickly diminished by the war, when work became a patriotic necessity. Yet wartime advisers in the magazines were careful to warn working girls from becoming "too mannish and ambitious in their jobs" (*Aunt Agony Advises*) for, when the victorious heroes came back to their former positions, women would have to return to domesticity. Thousands and thousands of women workers *were* dismissed and found no work to do. It was very hard on them. Everyone assumed that they would go quietly back to their homes, and that everything would be as it had been before.

Patriotism was not necessarily encouraged only in the area of non-domestic work. In *Woman's Life* (1915) a patriotic children's nurse was told in no uncertain terms that, while she was very anxious to leave the children she was looking after so that, as she said, she might serve 'Her King and Country':-

> "...it never seemed for a moment to occur to her that in helping to rear healthy children she was serving her King and Country, and in a very important way too. The little boys of today may be the soldiers of fifteen or twenty years hence. The little girls will be the mothers of the next generation."

Heroics were to be left to the men. However patriotic the magazine, girls were encouraged to look after their parents and continue with their domestic responsibilities, and not to rush into

64

enlistment. Those who did volunteer for work in the munitions industry, or the VADs, found the way was not made smooth for them. Quite the contrary, as Vera Brittain discovered:-

"I had an unsatisfactory sort of letter from the Red Cross, I noted one evening, talking vaguely of delays and numerous interviews. British authorities and their red tape are distinctly depressing. Strange that they should plead for volunteers and then make it as unpleasant as possible for you when you *have* volunteered."

Many girls and women accepted the risks of munitions work not only because they did not really understand the full dangers (as they later admitted) but out of a sense of patriotism:-

This extract was from *Tit Bits*, January 1916:

"Mary Ann: 'Please mum, I wish to give notice. My cousin has got me a place in a munitions factory.'

Mistress: 'Dear me, Mary! Well, of course you know that if you go dropping shells about as you do our crockery you won't remain long in your situation.'"

This was from *Our Girls* by Hall Caine:

"If anybody thinks the women working in such places are in fear of their lives he makes a woeful error. Let nobody be afraid to speak of the filling factories, or talk of them as places not proper for women. If that were so we should have to put men into them, for the work is necessary and urgent."

Ethel, however, did not have these feelings:

"Patriotism? I had a job and that was it."

Many middle class woman were encouraged to work by the euphoric, patriotic fervour which gripped the country in the first few

65

months of the war. As war charities increased, if paid work did not appeal they could knit socks, collect food, or raise money for war orphans: -

Dorothy: We went round the villages collecting eggs for wounded soldiers; there was a depot in the village. We gave children's concerts to raise money for wounded soldiers. We went from village to village."

Out of the Cage:

"It became almost a disgrace to be found at home; it required some justifying explanation. It was up to you to show that you were a patriotic worker all the time."

Woman's Life September 1914:

"It is simply splendid to see how readily our nation has responded to the call of her country... Everybody is busy and, best of all, everybody is working with a whole-hearted willingness."

"Last week we gave directions for the making of bedsocks. This week we illustrate a Balaclava Cap, with full working directions. It is needless to add how greatly these caps would be appreciated by our fighting men."

Tit Bits 1915:

"We are informed that there has recently been a falling off in the supplies of magazines and books to be sent to soldiers and sailors. We shall be glad, therefore, if our readers will endeavour to meet the needs of the men now fighting for their country by sending on all the magazines, books etc., which they can spare.

"Whether you have a brother, or a sweetheart, or a friend fighting with our gallant sailors or soldiers, you

cannot possibly please him more than by sending him half a dozen of the beautiful hem-stitched *Tit Bits* khaki handkerchiefs."

The press and posters reinforced these feelings, as can be seen in Chapter VII. Some of these were so evocative that their memory still remains:-

Grace: "I remember the war posters, particularly the Kitchener one – I can picture his face now."

The magazines were forceful in their exhortations:

"It is our business to pay when the Chancellor of the Exchequer knocks at the door with his little account rendered for expenses incurred in dealing with the enemy; it is our privilege and our pleasure to give when the Spirit of Humanity seeks audience, as he does now." (*Vogue* 1916)

War Rules for Housewives

1. Conduct the shopping personally. Estimate as far as possible the requirements of each meal, as the markets fluctuate daily.
2. If possible, carry the parcels home to save horses and men needed for other purposes.
3. Choose those foods which give most nourishment for the least money.
4. Do not take in more milk than you know you will require.
5. Brown all crusts and scraps of bread in the oven; crush and place in air-tight tins: to be used instead of flour in making puddings.
6. Do not cut any bread until it is at least one day old.
7. Keep all cold vegetables left over from dinner for salads for next day.
8. Do not make more tea than is likely to be used.
9. Avoid all luxuries.

Although some of these contemporary accounts could be seen as propaganda, and many women jumped into the war effort because of criticism if they did not, or because their friends were already contributing, others said they enjoyed their work, partly because they really did think they were supporting the 'war to end all wars'.

GIVE, GIVE, GIVE: the public was constantly exhorted. SAVE, SAVE, SAVE. When a million young men had given up their own civilian freedom and comfort to go soldiering, it seemed only right that those civilians who remained at home should dig deep into their pockets and purses to provide them with comforts, and with all the care that money could provide when they came back wounded. When soldiers were prepared to risk their lives, it was surely not too much to ask that people at home should sacrifice the luxury of meat on just one day a week, should save fuel by giving up their motor cars, economise on light by retiring to bed an hour earlier, and that women should assist in saving raw materials, badly needed for uniforms and blankets, by adopting the new short skirt.

Taken to the extreme, however, patriotism swung towards jingoism. There were some displays of war hysteria, some empty rhetoric in the recruiting speeches, some women who presented white feathers on the streets to men of military age not in uniform:-

"I saw one man given a white feather – unfair – as people did not really know what others' circumstances were." (Jane)

"My brother was given a white feather before he was eighteen. Next term he left school and enlisted. He would not go into the army – felt he was too young to be in command of men. Learnt to fly, rather than wishing to kill anyone." (Betty)

Sometimes feelings of hatred against the Germans seemed to be extreme:-

"In a munitions factory, I speak to two educated women, who turn out to be High School mistresses from a town that has been several times visited by Zeppelins. 'We just felt

we must come and help kill Germans,' they say quietly."
(*Out of the Cage*)

Yet lack of information in the press, and the resulting rumours that were bound to circulate, must have helped to reinforce these feelings of needing to do something positive. Vera Brittain noted how difficult it was to know what was really happening:-

> "As usual the press had given no hint of that (Neuve Chapelle) tragedy's dimensions, and it was only through the long casualty lists, and the persistent demoralising rumour that owing to a miscalculation in time thousands of our men had been shot down by our own guns, that the world was gradually coming to realise something of what the engagement had been."

Memories of a VAD who found life in a hospital 'the happiest time I have spent' are for the most part in complete contrast with the pictures drawn by most of the literature that appeared retrospectively after the war (as shown in Chapter VIII). However, awareness of their part in the war made some women think very carefully about the implications of the work they did. Their friends and relatives were dying at the Front, yet they were helping to make shells to kill other men:

> "So on the whole my experience, such as it has been, in a munitions factory has been a bright and happy one. Only for the fact that I am using my lifes [sic] energy to destroy human souls gets on my nerves. Yet on the other hand, I am doing what I can to bring this horrible affair to an end."
> (*Out of the Cage*)

There was much distrust by authority and middle class people – as in Victorian times – of working class women. They were held to be in need of moral education and guidance and young women in the factory were to be organised into clubs and classes and taught to be quiet, obedient workers. Working mothers also had to be watched, to make sure they did not neglect their children for their work – or their work for their children. The war intensified this mistrust and brought

70

in new fears about women's morals. Concern was expressed that long hours working with men, journeys to and from work at night, and the existence of huge numbers of soldiers in barracks in nearby towns, would all lead to a rising tide of immorality and illegitimacy:-

> "War-time hysterics gave currency to fabulous rumour. From press and pulpit stories ran rampant of drunkenness and depravity amongst the women of the masses. Alarmist morality mongers conceived most monstrous visions of girls and women... burdening the country with swarms of illegitimate infants." (*Out of the Cage*)

> "That the gravest moral evil must all too often be the outcome of this working together of men and women is obvious."

This second comment, from *The Englishwoman* January 1919, is in direct contrast to the mainly radical viewpoint of this magazine.

Middle class women probably experienced more changes in their day-to-day lives than did working class women. Young women were out late at night, were unchaperoned, and lived in hostels and lodgings that they would never have seen in ordinary circumstances. Yet there was no sign that they produced thousands of new babies, in spite of discussion in the press and in political life:-

> "A root idea for a war baby article... If Tommy was a decent fellow he abstained because he didn't want to leave his girl in trouble... If he wasn't he chanced it because it might be his last chance..." (Ford Madox Ford – *Parade's End*)

A leading article in *The Times*, dealing 'with both sides of the question', remarked that this was a case for sense and charity:-

> "While we must not condone the offence, we must not make its results worse by harsh and narrow treatment... We must condemn the sin and the sinners while yet

remarking that the results of it can be made the useful citizens of tomorrow."

The beginning of the storm had been the discovery in April 1915 of 'War Babies'. In a letter to the *Morning Post*, which was intensively quoted and added to in the rest of the press, a Conservative MP, Mr Ronald McNeill, announced that throughout the country, in districts where large numbers of troops had been quartered a 'great number of girls' were about to become unmarried mothers. The topic was a godsend for journalists and for the letter-writing public. For two weeks even the *Observer* devoted a great deal of space to it, but on the third week the editor peevishly snapped that the 'whole matter had been grossly exaggerated'. There was justification for the *Observer*'s embarrassment: the year 1915 actually presented the highly moral combination of an exceptionally low illegitimate birth rate and phenomenally high marriage rate. The marriage rate in 1914 had been 15.9 per thousand. In 1915 it rose to 19.4 per thousand – the attitude probably being to get married while there was the chance. 200,000 people were married in the first phase of the war. Between 1916 and 1918 the rate fell to 13.8 per thousand. Between 1919 and 1920 the rate rose again to 20.2 per thousand, as those who had served returned home. By 1916 the illegitimacy rate did go up, and by the end of the war it was about 30% up on pre-war.

The exact reality behind the stories and the statistics is difficult to determine, but obviously it sprang from two related circumstances: changed conditions at home, especially for women, as we have seen, and the new awareness, in face of the slaughter on the battlefields, of the transience of human life. "Give the boys on leave a good time" was the universal sentiment at home, and the good time consisted to a very large extent in consuming alcohol and enjoying sex. As a popular song of the period had it: 'There's a girl for every soldier'.

Certainly, some soldiers took advantage of wartime 'romances' and left some women literally holding the baby, although there is no mention of this in any of the magazines under discussion. Yet, given the tensions of war and the speedy changes in social and sexual barriers, restraint was, in fact, remarkable.

As a result of what was seen to be happening, the Government decided that those women suspected of drinking or consorting with men other than their husbands were to be investigated and their separation allowances stopped if convicted of any such offence. A new Women's Police Patrol was formed to help to enforce these regulations. This was noted in *The Englishwoman* of January 1919:-

> "... the presence of women police does a great deal and their warnings and remonstrances are often extraordinarily efficacious in recalling both men and girls to a sense of what they owe to themselves and each other."

Marriages were bound to be put under strain, and there were certainly affairs, pregnancies and separations as a result of the stress of war. It is hard, however, to discover what people really thought about changes in their relationships because this was not something people were willing to discuss openly. In the magazines, in both the fiction and in the articles, as will be seen, fidelity was taken for granted and happy endings were inevitable; there was complete absence of discussion of marital problems.

1917-1918 was almost certainly the hardest year of the war for civilians. The hardships of austerity were made grimmer by the intensification of German bombing raids. The worst raid of the whole war came on 13th June, 1917, when 162 people were killed and 432 injured, and the autumn that followed was so full of menace that Londoners took to the practice of sheltering in the Underground. Between January 1915 and April 1918 there were fifty-one Zeppelin raids, causing 1,913 casualties, and between December 1914 and June 1918 there were fifty-seven aeroplane raids, causing 2,907 casualties. All in all, air raid casualties during the war totalled 1,117 killed and 2,886 injured.

A young VAD St John's Ambulance nurse was brought very close to the war by a Zeppelin raid on Hull in June 1915. On the night of the Hull raid she attempted to write an account of it and catch some of the immediacy of her experience. The Germans dropped thirteen high explosive and thirty-nine incendiary bombs, killing twenty-four people and injuring forty. Grace remembers the Zeppelins flying low, picked out with searchlights 'like some beast in the sky'. Jane remembers an air raid warning during the day, but nothing happened. That same night an aerial torpedo fell on the railway line between Cricklewood Lane and Mill Lane, West Hampstead, missing the factory where she worked, but breaking all the windows on both sides of the railway

74

line. She was shaken by the explosion on the railway line, as she was on the iron bridge across the line, but not hurt:-

> "I got up and ran the rest of the way home, to find my sister had put a table in front of the fireplace, with bedding on top – but had forgotten about the chimney – and they were covered in soot!"

Life was made harsher by the 'flu epidemic which swept across Europe, attacking a population which was weakened by three years of strain, tension, grief, hard work and a limited diet. The epidemic reached its height by the end of 1918, and produced a new outbreak during the first three months of 1919. Coming at that moment it added greatly to human misery. In England and Wales 150,000 people died from it, more than 15,000 of them in London alone. Dorothy Moriarty described her experience of it:-

> "I was working in one of our two military wards. One of my patients was Private Watkins, in Bed 7. He had come home on compassionate leave, and was due to return to the Front when he fell victim to Spanish 'flu. He was a civilian who had volunteered in the early days during the wave of patriotism that swept the country. He had come through the hell across the Channel unscathed – only to face this."

People grew angry about high rents, bad housing and food shortages and these, together with industrial unrest, and fears of Bolshevism – for this was the time of the height of the Russian Revolution – forced the government to introduce food rationing and a national economy campaign.

Voluntary rationing had been introduced on 3rd February, 1917. Each citizen was to restrict himself to four pounds of bread or three pounds of flour, two and a half pounds of meat, and three quarters of a pound of sugar per week. Compulsion was held in the background as a threat which could be applied if necessary, and supervisory powers were vested in local Food Committees. Yet the scheme had no basis in reality; the poor still ate far more bread and far less meat than provided for here, and sugar was already almost unobtainable in many places. The magazines followed the government lead:-

"If coal is not to go up to famine prices and the rather shorter supplies held by merchants are to last until next spring the strictest economy must be exercised in regard to its use." *Tit Bits* January 1916.

"In Goodall's Egg Powder there exists one of the best wartime kitchen helps you can desire. It will save you three-fourths of the cost of eggs, yet give you (even with the present flour) cakes of the most perfect quality and richness and flavour." *Woman's Life* December 1918.

Vera Brittain felt no sense of joy when peace finally arrived:-

"All those with whom I had really been intimate were gone; not one remained to share with me the heights and depths of my memories."

She had lost all the men most dear to her. Other bereaved parents, wives and children felt similarly stunned. The main feeling was one of relief that at last people could return to normal living. Vera Brittain continued:-

"When the sound of victorious guns burst over London at 11 a.m. on November 11th, 1918, the men and women who looked incredulously into each other's faces did not cry jubilantly: 'We've won the War!' They only said: 'The War is over.'"

Rose had a similar memory:-

"On Armistice Day, I remember the open buses, the American and English soldiers, shouting and excited. *The feeling of relief.*"

Dorothy continues her story about Private Watkins:-

"The morning dragged on. And then, suddenly, it seemed as if every church bell in the great city went mad –

the same bells that had been silent for four years. The Armistice had been signed. The war was over. I looked at Private Watkins. Had I imagined the flicker in his glazed eyes? I picked up his hand. There was no pulse to be found..."

The radical changes in society that had taken place as a result of the war should have continued when peace came. By 1918 nearly 5,000,000 women held paid employment. Women's wartime jobs and the break-down of class barriers in the factory and at the Front, and the possibility of growing political awareness in the working class to help demand better jobs, housing and pay was noted in the *New Statesman*:-

> "They appear more alert, more critical of the conditions under which they work, more ready to make a stand against injustice than their pre-war selves. They have a keener appetite for experience and pleasure and a tendency quite new to their class to protest against wrongs even before they become intolerable."

Woman's Life December 1918 confirmed this viewpoint:-

> "During the war women from all grades of society have met and worked side by side. They have arrived at a better understanding of each other and have realised how the 'other half of the world lives'. A new spirit of oneness has been awakened... she is more confident and self-reliant; in a word, she has found herself, and when the task of reconstruction is begun this alert, live, united Womanhood will be a force with which to reckon."

Yet, at the end of the war, women were again forced to return to jobs in domestic service, or to work within their own homes, as there was little other work available. *My Weekly* of August 1918 was already anticipating this peacetime reversal:-

> "Three years ago I came to the office of Messrs J. Raymond & Son, cotton brokers, to act as book-keeper in

the place of John Bryant, who had 'joined up'... And now the war is over, and Sergeant Bryant is coming back. I can hand him over the reins with thankfulness that I have done my bit and stood to the guns and I am also proud because I know that when Sergeant Bryant returns to 'civvy life' he will find his books in order."

Some women left their jobs willingly, but it would appear that not everyone was intimidated by attempts to persuade them to give up their independence:-

Ethel: "After the war, I would not go back into service; I went to work in a pub – I was not allowed to talk to the customers."

Sybil: "There was no problem about taking over jobs. Some did not step back when the men returned."

The war had given them a taste of a different life, and putting the clock back proved difficult. However, many married women with children whose husbands had returned to civilian life were often relieved to abandon such a strenuous existence, while most middle class munitions workers had no intention of remaining in such work beyond the war. By 1919 women's unemployment numbers dropped dramatically, to about 29,000 by November of that year. Many had been systematically pushed off the unemployment register and been forced to give up paid work altogether, or to take work in the unpopular 'women's trades', especially domestic service and laundry. This was a calculated action taken by the government and its agents, the labour exchanges, and backed up by an unpleasant and hysterical campaign in the national and local press:-

"It was pointed out to them that their first duty was to the soldier – the man who had done his bit for the past four years – and who would now be wanting to return to his normal occupation." (*Out of the Cage*)

The Englishwoman January, 1919, agreed:-

> "They themselves would be the last to expect or even to desire that the mobilised men whose places they filled should not be reinstated upon their return, and they also fully recognise the claims of the skilled men who trained them in their work."

The daily press complained increasingly that women were not returning to domestic service; certainly the attacks on women revolved around two themes: "They should not be hanging on to 'men's jobs' and should give way to soldiers, and secondly, they should not be unemployed because there were really plenty of jobs available to them." *(Out of the Cage)*. By 1920 more than four million men had been released from the services. Reabsorption of most of them into civil employment was made possible by the economic boom of 1919, and by discharging the women from jobs in industry to make way for them.

Once again, the myth of the apathetic, docile woman, who lacked ambition and would willingly accept lower pay than men, resurfaced and remained an enduring one. The magazines helped to reinforce the return to their pre-war non-status, apart from the more radical magazines, such as *The Englishwoman*:-

> "...they demand that they should have a fair field, rightly considering that their continued employment in industries in which they have gained valuable experience, and in which they have proved themselves efficient, should not be regarded as a favour."

Home Chat January 1919, too, saw a definite leaning towards recognition of change:-

> "Wives with independent means are happier as a rule than wives who have no money of their own. The moneyless woman is at a disadvantage in married life. Therefore, if for family reasons a woman CANNOT pursue her career, let it be recognised that by staying at home and keeping house she is EARNING A SALARY, and she should receive it."

There is an evident suggestion here of a more feminist approach.

Post-war women, having gained more freedom with the vote - although this was only for women over thirty until 1928 - shorter skirts and financial independence, no longer presented themselves as delicate 'hot house flowers' - nor were they treated as such; the magazines reinforcing the need to realise how "Times have changed, as you must know, and in these days, when women claim equality with men, it is only right that they should be taken at their own valuation" (*Aunt Agony Advises*). The new freedom due to the rise in women's wages during and after the war was first enjoyed by the working class girl, the reader of magazines such as *Tit Bits, The Red Rose, Peg's Paper* or *Forget Me Not*. The immediately post-war batch of 'mill girl publications' such as these were unlike their pre war counterparts, which had been heartily maternal towards their readers - mother/friend. The new crop of 'aunties', in an attempt to reach their higher wage earning, more independent readers, tried to appear as chums: -

> "My name is Peg, and my one aim in life is to give you a really cheery paper like nothing you've ever read before. Not so long ago, I was a mill girl too. Because I've been a worker, too, and know what girls like, I'm going to give you a paper you'll enjoy... look on me as a real helper. I will try to advise you on any problem." (*Aunt Agony Advises*)

The change in middle class attitudes to women working outside the home, and the resulting emancipation of the middle class girl, proved a lengthier process. Her education was more extended, and her infrequent opportunities for earning enough to support herself were considerably fewer than that of the working class girl. The problem pages recognised, however, that the earning power of the 'new woman' had given her an unprecedented independence, and the tone of their advice moved away from the traditional 'motherly' type of support.

Just as the troops anticipated returning to a 'land fit for heroes', so many women thought that they would be in some way rewarded for their wartime services. The immediate consequence of demobilisation, however, was unemployment and for some a return to domesticity. Despite this, however, not every woman automatically gave up her job, for the loss of so many men meant a shortage of husbands and breadwinners. Yet the magazines, aided and abetted by pressure from the increasingly competitive world of advertising, offered to the working girl a fantasy world of a husband, a home to keep tidy and children, with an increasing emphasis on domestic economy, knitting and homemaking; all areas which have remained uppermost in the magazines to the present day.

In these two chapters we have observed the world of the magazines via the changes in fashion, morals and manners, and contrasted these changes with the reality of the world of work in women's lives in the First World War. Looking at the features in the magazines in more detail will point to the propagandist element in wartime, and yet show once again the difference between the image displayed and the reality of women's wartime lives.

MISTAKES I See at **DANCES:**

Ho...
Ch...
AND MO...

By a Girl who
goes to a
great many
*(See
Page 34.)*

THIS
IS
WRONG!

(See Page 34.)

Vol. XCVI. No. 1243.   TWOPENCE.   JANUARY 11th, 1913.

CHAPTER IV

Women at Home – Putting Their Message Across:

"The women at home can in their own way be of just as much service as the man at the Front. Think how encouraging it must be to every soldier and sailor to know that the women at home are working so eagerly in order to give them as much comfort as possible when they are called upon to suffer."

The magazines turn the mirror which reflects social change towards the world at different times, and then reflect the messages they receive back to their readers. They produce what they think their readers are thinking, and what will sell. Their readers pick up the messages and reflect them back again. The agenda is, therefore, set by both producer and consumer; and the magazines therefore contain elements which are both realistic and idealistic. An examination of the range of features in some examples of the magazines will pinpoint many similarities and differences in these two-way messages.

Home Chat, which cost 1d in 1915, 2d in 1919, tended to adopt a light-hearted style of writing. It did not appear to involve itself in the deeper social and personal issues raised in some of the other magazines, but seemed to be more preoccupied by the surface of things, such as issues of manners:-

> "Mistakes I see at Dances – never wear a big-brimmed hat to an afternoon dance. It is wrong, and most uncomfortable, besides the fact that the brim is apt to knock one's partner's head every few minutes. Don't wear, when dancing, a sash with long ends, especially if it is finished with beaded tassels... they are apt to catch in other people's frocks as they pass."

or less conventional romantic issues:-

> "Ruth is more than seven years older than her husband, and as she's one of the happiest of married women, I persuaded her one evening to tell me, for the benefit of my girl friends, a little about the courtship days and the

85

When He Proposed.

It isn't often you can get a girl to talk about "When He Proposed," is it? But the writer of this series managed to persuade some of her married friends to "recall sweet memories." And very interesting reading I think you will find them.

No. 6.—THE JUNIOR PARTNER.

YOU know I always believed strongly that the woman should take 'an older than herself." Doesn't Shakespeare put it that way, more or less? Anyway, I was most emphatic on the point."

Ruth is more than seven years older than her husband, and as she's one of the happiest of married women, I persuaded her one evening to tell me, for the benefit of my girl friends, a little about the courtship days and the proposal.

"But, you know, when the real right man comes along you're apt to forget your theories. You fall so deep in love that you just forget that, according to your pet principle, this man is decidedly ruled out.

"Really, Harold must have thought me very absurd when he proposed to me. Of course, I loved him right enough, but in a sudden fit of shyness my forgotten and vanished theory came stammering to my tongue. But think of the disparity, I began. Harold looked downright mad. 'Think of the fiddlesticks!' he said. 'Do you love me or don't you?'

"I laughed.

"'That cornered you, didn't it?'

"A bit, I admitted it, though I forget just what I said. Perhaps it was just the way I looked. Anyhow, Harold seemed relieved. 'Oh!' he said, 'that's better.' I began to think I was mistaken when you talked of disparities. Disparity!'—the word seemed quite to disgust him—'What is it you're frightening yourself about?'"

"So I suppose you told him?"

"Yes, I said a lot about women ageing so much sooner than men, and that he'd find me old and dull and dowdy while he was still a gay young spark."

Ruth laughed, a pleasant, light-hearted laugh.

"You'd have been amused if you'd heard him," she continued. "I always say he scolded

"But think of the disparity,' I began. Harold looked downright mad. Think of the fiddlesticks!' he said. 'Do you love me or don't you?'

me into marrying him. You know he's so full of common sense; he just talked away patiently, explaining to me how times had changed, and how, nowadays, men entered earlier into life's arena, and fought a keener battle, so that at forty most of them were bald or grey or worn-looking. And he protested that they didn't want dolls or kittenish schoolgirls to giggle by the fireside at home, but sensible, kindly women fit to be helpmates.'

"Ruth laughed again.

"'Sounds awfully stodgy, doesn't it? But the dear lad was so terribly in earnest. I believe I cried at the time, though I've often laughed at him since. Then he pointed out that a girl who faced the realities of life, as we do in these modern days, kept her heart and mind young if she was the right sort of girl. 'And you're the right sort for me, and I mean to marry you,' he ended up, in his masterful way. You know how tall and strong he is. Well, he just picked me up in his arms and kissed me. 'All right, Harold,' I said, 'I'll risk it.' Anyway, I can always look up to you. We both laughed, like the pair of happy children we were, for all my seven years of seniority, and we've never let the thought of those said seven years worry us in the least.'"

"Then Harold was right?"

"Facts have proved him a prophet. I spend my time growing younger day by day. He makes me so gloriously happy. And though he's not showing signs of baldness yet, still, he isn't such an irresponsible party that he finds me deadly dull. So altogether," she laughed, "I'm remarkably glad I took that risk, for it isn't a disparity of years that breaks up a home. Tell your girls that the thing to be avoided is a disparity in heart and mind and outlook. The years between don't count where love and trust are dwelling together. That's the long and the short of it."

THE END.

proposal – 'Tell your girls that the thing to be avoided is a disparity in heart and mind and outlook. The years between don't count where love and trust are dwelling together'."

Home Chat contained one or two serials, one or two complete stories, between ten to twenty features (in wartime, heavily propagandist), three or four cookery or domestic features, and a short religious tract. *Woman's Life* was very similar in layout, though it contained more articles on beauty problems, and a mother's question page. Its price also went up during the war from 1d to 2d. The shortage of paper in wartime was bound to affect the price of the magazines. Many newspapers, as well, shrank in size and were printed upon paper of various qualities and shades.

My Weekly contained more fiction (three or four stories), but was the same price. In *My Weekly*, however, the more 'realistic' stories hinted at a certain recognition of every day experience and difficulty, and from identification with this followed the readers' desire to complete the story, to see how such issues were resolved. *My Weekly* moved from a base of home and family with the reader addressed as wife and mother. Yet the editorials also drew on wider, more worldly issues, brought into the area of home. As with the other magazines mentioned above, the same rules or convictions which were used in the outside world were being advised as solutions for inside the home; asserting the importance of the home. There appeared to be contradictory pressure on women between femininity and domesticity on the one hand, and individualism on the other.

These magazines were written to a simple classic formula of romantic fiction, household hints, cookery and dressmaking, a children's feature, and advice on personal problems, interwoven with news and gossip, and introduced with a 'plain talk' from the editor. They appealed to the mass female market and thus provided the best basis for future expansion. *My Weekly*, in particular, enjoyed considerable success and, as will be shown, is still in print. Its editorial policy of getting into an active and intimate relationship with its readers has since been copied by many successful magazine weeklies, and its adherence to a simple, home-centred formula indicated the direction which an increasing number of women's magazines were to take in the years between the wars.

The success achieved by magazines such as *My Weekly* showed that the interests and activities of the majority of women were still, after the war, centred upon the home, and that their attitudes concerning their social role had been largely unaffected by the campaign to extend women's rights, or the social upheavals and changed roles during the war.

Tit Bits appeared to be aimed at a different market – that of family entertainment – from that of the women's magazines, whose traditionally narrow range – fiction, home, cooking, fashion features, letters and 'personal problems' – was aimed at 'the world of women'. Although the same price as these others, the fiction (two stories) was heavily outweighed by the features, of which there were ten pages, as well as 'bits' from books and magazines, jokes, competitions and letters, some of which raised problems. In complete contrast, *Vogue* and *The Englishwoman* were in an entirely different style, with the use of more complicated vocabulary and literary allusion, and far less appearance of direct communication with their readers. In the stories and features content, a far greater range of subjects appeared. In particular there were articles by well-known politicians, businessmen and journalists of the period under discussion, aiming at stimulating public debate, as well as much concern with current feminist political discussion in *The Englishwoman* and fashion, art and drama in *Vogue*. *The Englishwoman* contained no advertisements. *Vogue* had crossed the Atlantic from America in 1916, and added new colour and vitality to the publishing scene. For one shilling (5p) it offered 120 glossy pages fortnightly, plus a colour supplement, and it covered a wide range of subjects beside fashion, including society news, entertainment, cultural and discussion features of a high literary standard. The editor justified the policy of intellectual challenge by reference to the philosophy underlying women's publishing in America:-

"America believes in the higher education of women as does no other country on earth. She knows perfectly well that marriage and motherhood, paramount as they are, are not to be the whole of this girl's life... a woman of this class doesn't spend the whole twenty-four hours of her day rocking her baby and making a good man happy... Do we realise it in England?"

Yet women's magazines still confined themselves almost entirely to servicing women in their domestic role, and paid little attention to the possibilities of widening their sphere of influence. Taking an active part in life outside the home was never presented as a desirable extension of a woman's sphere, nor was the practicability of combining the roles of wife and worker ever properly investigated.

Editorially, the women's magazines tailored their content to fit what they felt were the needs and interests of their readers. They set the overall style of address to their readers: a friendly conversational style of one woman to another; the concerned friend of the woman reader who addressed her in personal, not collective terms. This apparently intimate communication between editors and readers contributed to the sense, for the reader, of entering a 'woman's world' common to the editor and herself alike. The friendly editorial voice also offered a reassurance that this was a friend the reader could rely on and trust. Readers could make intimate confessions to this friend, who was also the authoritative expert. The 'auntie' replied as the concerned but perhaps older and wiser friend, writing, particularly in wartime, as in *Home Chat* 1915, as follows:-

"Week by week the old proverb, 'Necessity is the mother of invention' comes more to the fore. You HAVE to be inventive in war time. Burn the bottom out of your kettle by leaving it on the gas and forgetting all about it, and the man who mends it might be making shells or rifles if it weren't for you."

"Spring cleaning this year has taught the mistress of a home to rely more upon herself – to lay carpets and lino, to drive a screw in a loose door handle. Daring spirits have papered whole rooms and enamelled the bath with meticulous pride!"

The magazines were not entirely an homogeneous group, either with regard to their contents, or the way they addressed their readers. The working class magazines were more motherly, the middle class more sisterly, though the distinction became less wide after the war. The editorial philosophy of the weekly magazines which became popular between the First and Second World Wars moved to a simple but revolutionary concept: the entertainment and enlightenment of working class women was *extended* into areas of interest and expertise previously found more noticeably in the middle class journals. Yet the rapidly expanding variety of consumer goods and technological advances for home improvement, which were advertised and examined, could not be afforded by the majority of their readers. To offer a comparison, in 1906 a vacuum cleaner had cost £35 – the same number of weeks' wages for working people. By 1939, a refrigerator was still 24 guineas (25 4s) and by this time £3 a week was seen as a very good wage. Like the fiction in the magazines, consumer goods held out a promise of what 'might' be, rather than what 'was' attainable.

In the First World War women had no 'voice'; the vote had not yet been granted to them, nor was their wartime role as organised and quickly defined as in the Second World War. Yet editorial policy in the magazines of this period contained similar exhortations to those of 1939. In *Woman's Life* September 1914, the editor exhorted:-

> "The women at home can in their own way be of just as much service as the men at the Front. Think how encouraging it must be to every soldier and sailor to know that the women at home are working so eagerly in order to give them as much comfort as possible when they are called upon to suffer."

In the Second World War women's magazines took on a new social significance and political direction. Their potential influence over their readers and their unique ability to address themselves to both private and public female activities was quickly recognised and used by the British government, and the magazines became the 'voice' of women in wartime. *Weldon's Ladies Journal*, for example, stated:-

> "Now we have been at war for several weeks. Our lives have left the quiet, privileged backwaters of peace, and have now to stem the hazardous and unruly tide of war. We are only just at the beginning... but I want to assure you that WLJ will set itself to help the women of this country,

90

whether their jobs are at home or afield, to keep a cheerful heart and to maintain a calm competence."

"Nothing – not even National Service – is of more vital importance than home-making and homekeeping. On it, the whole of our future depends." (*Woman and Home*)

Both of the magazines are quoted in *Women in Wartime (1939-1945)* by Jane Waller and Michael Vaughan-Rees.

There is, therefore, an overall pattern to the way in which women's magazines put together their features and articles, and this pattern produces a series of solutions for the reader. Editorials of women's magazines are a good guide to the voice of the magazine, setting its style and tone of address to the reader. They are also likely to represent the social attitudes within which a magazine is operating. Similarly, the readers' letters selected for publication are likely to highlight the issues the magazine thinks are the concern of its readers. Thus the exceptional discretionary powers of the editors – agenda setters to the female world – are both active and prescriptive:-

"Violet, dear, I fear your story is one of many, and it ends in either of two ways. The 'young man' sows a few wild oats and learns to recognise the difference between false and true affection, or he gives way altogether and becomes fickle and worthless. I hope that the first will take place with your boy, but you must not think of interfering as things are. It would be most unwise, and would never do." *Woman's Life*, September 1914.

"Although I was badly treated by my first boyfriend when I was sixteen, my fiancé couldn't be more considerate. He spends hours reassuring me that he loves everything about me, yet I just have to see him glance at another woman..." "You must work to rebuild your self-esteem. No evidence exists. It's only you speaking negatively to yourself and *you* can put that right." *My Weekly*, 1989.

The 'voice of authority' does not appear to have changed over the years!

Beneath the description of 'general service and entertainment' of the magazines, is a hidden 'mix' of *women's work* and the subsequent need for the purchase of commodities in the areas of both domesticity and beauty. These areas are bound within a framework that seeks to entertain and provide women with pleasure.

Although there are individual differences between them, all women's magazines have this balance in common. For example, in discussion and representation of paid work, the magazines being examined tended to harmonise paid work with domestic life. The magazines omitted what were, in their terms, the seedier aspects of paid work, like industrial conflicts or the marital and familial problems that working women had to cope with. The world of work was shown within the context of a 'fantasy' world of entertainment, rather than the serious responsibility of a career. (*Woman's Life*, July 1915):-

> "Carmine Silver – it's a pretty name, isn't it? And when I see it now on hoardings and bus tops, and glittering outside the theatre, it reminds me of those early days when two devoted parents cared for me, and watched over me, and stinted themselves, so that I might have the things I needed... they would go out together to do their work, leaving me to experiment with rouge and powder, and dream of the days when I too should 'make them worship me.'"

The magazines suggested that work offered the choice of what you wanted to do and merely going ahead and doing it. The definition of paid work was highly selective. Dirty, boring, unsatisfying, extremely badly paid – the kind of work women did on a factory production line or as a domestic servant, i.e. working class jobs – never appeared in the magazines. Ethel has described her life as a domestic servant (page 39), and her long journeys to and from the Woolwich Arsenal (page 41). Here she gives her description of her wartime job:-

"I found it strange in the Arsenal because I had to do sewing! I had to weigh the cordite and balastite (?) and put it into bags, which went behind the shells and was forced out when they were fired. I was paid according to what the munitions shop produced."

The stress on women as individuals, who are *shown* to be in a position to choose – whether it is paid work or the type of curtains for the living room – is an important strand in women's magazines. It covers up the reality of the pressures of work and family which act against choice being a possibility. As previously shown, responsibility versus individuality is one of the recurring themes in women's magazines.

The area of domestic responsibility for the home – shopping, cooking, housework, home making – consistently remained at the centre of the magazines. Domesticity, linked with consumption, was and still is constructed round pleasure and work. Differences between men and women were acknowledged in the magazines; differences between classes were not, except implicitly. This was made easier by one of the characteristics of 'femininity', which presented itself as classless. *All* women were considered to be potential mothers or housewives: 'women are women the world over'. The kind of domestic practice and knowledge which was advocated for women presented itself as the normal and natural one. The act of attributing certain feminine qualities to all women – making them seem natural, normal and universal for women – also tended to conceal the existence of class difference. The effect of this was that the magazines gave the illusion of classlessness in the representation of domesticity. Yet this representation in the magazines was heavily class coded. It was, on the one hand, an uneven combination of a middle class lifestyle – as in the home and cooking features – and on the other hand a reproduction of a lower middle class lifestyle and culture in the articles and documentary features, for example in *Home Chat* of 1915:-

"The truth about carrying parcels home is, of course, that we ought to think ourselves exceedingly lucky to have the parcels to carry. One grocer mentioned at a recent meeting that when his son enlisted, he put up a notice in the shop asking customers to remember that if they were not as promptly attended to as usual, it was because a member of the staff was serving them in another capacity. 'Since then,' he said, 'many more ladies than before have carried home their parcels.'"

"It gave me a surprise the other day, while having tea with friends on the outskirts, when a little girl called 'to mend the baby's push cart'. She set to work with workmanlike capability... she was only thirteen, she told me. She had picked up her skill in watching her father and brothers at work. Her brothers had left the shop to join the Army and Miss Thirteen is her father's right hand now." (*Home Chat*, 1915, also.)

The avoidance of the word 'sex' was very obvious in the magazines. Various words were used by the authors of the letters to suggest sex (readers' letters were edited and substitution may have been used by the editors). These euphemisms and the advice to 'write to me on any problems on which you hesitate to seek the advice of your friends' indicated the delicacy and embarrassment for women of discussing and reading about sexual matters. The letters in the magazines also revealed that sexuality was not a topic which was easily discussed between couples and families (*Home Chat*, July 1915):-

"At one time, not so very long ago, either, it wasn't thought quite 'nice' for a woman to have decided opinions about things – the vital things that concern life and love and marriage. It betrayed a sad lack of delicacy to discuss such matters, however nearly they affected you... In these days, when women are everywhere 'holding their own', when it has been proved that they can be just as practical and dependable and loyal as men, an intellectual companionship has sprung up between the two sexes unthought of in the old days. Very few men now imagine that 'all a woman wants is to be made love to', and women no longer have the feeling that nearly all other women will suspect them of ulterior motives if they dare to show even the most ordinary friendliness to one of the opposite sex."

Sybil agreed with this viewpoint:-

"The sexual attitudes shown in the magazines were very traditional and rigid – but I am still."

The social position of the reader can generate different sorts of reading and interpretation. The place of reading may differ, alone or amongst others. The reader may be looking specifically for a recipe or a pattern, or a temporary means of escape from daily routine. The possible contexts for reading the magazines would be endlessly variable, and would affect both *what* is read and *how* it is read. Dorothy, Grace, Susan and Doris gave their opinions about the magazines:-

"I read magazines like *Tit Bits* and occasionally *Vogue*. We had *Pearson's Weekly*, and did the competitions. I imagined myself dressed in the clothes in *Vogue* – I had ½p a week to spend."

"*My Weekly* was very popular, particularly the competitions. I liked the serials and recipes and fashions, and how to bring up children, and how to make jam. And I read *Girl's Friend*. I read magazines to forget what was happening. We were all great readers in my family."

"My mother took *Home Chat* and I read it. I liked the letters pages, though I did not agree with the advice."

"I remember *My Weekly*, *Home Chat* and *Letters* and *Tit Bits*. I read comics as well. I liked the fashions and cooking. I was a good sewer, so I copied the patterns for my doll. I read the agony columns, to have a good laugh. Writing about men knocking them about and giving them babies every year. Silly things they asked!"

Mary, Elizabeth, Rose, Betty and Sybil also gave their opinions:-

"I remember *My Weekly*. I liked waiting for the serials each week, and the 'funny bits', and the problem pages – it was only a few coppers. We passed them on, one to another."

"I remember some of the magazines. I made my own clothes, and was very fond of cooking – my mother taught me."

"I can remember the pictures in the magazines. I used to look at the children's pages, and the fashions, in *Home Chat*. I remember *Peg's Paper*, and also read *Answers* and *Tit Bits*. I liked the romantic stories."

"I remember reading the *Illustrated London News* for the pictures, *Vogue* for the fashions, *Home Chat* for the stories."

"I read the magazines, but not the serials. I read the problem pages. The magazines did bring the war home, but a lot was suppressed as well. I was not affected by what I read in the magazines. It was an escape as things were difficult. The information was useful on fashion, health, recreation, ideas for the home. The fiction was a fantasy world. The magazines did deal with the consequences of the war – e.g. eggless cakes. The stories always ended happily."

As we can see from the above opinions, how much of the magazine is read and how often, will also determine the reader's overall view of the magazine. Most readings would be selective, through choice of what is read and how it is read.

The reader is socially placed before beginning to read the magazine. The act of reading is never passive, however, but brings to bear on the text – consciously or unconsciously – knowledge of other texts, knowledge of the reader's culture, experience of the reader's social position. Age, class, education, work and political experience, the area in which the reader lives, all determine what meaning is made of any feature or story. Each reader will have a different experience of and perspective on the various topics in the magazine. These factors would inevitably shape how an item is read. Therefore, although the editors, producers and writers of a magazine may intend to convey particular meanings, they cannot, obviously, guarantee that the readers will interpret any feature in any particular way. Nevertheless, a combination of cultural and 'common sense' factors, codes of representation – with which both staff and readers are familiar – make it likely that a preferred dominant meaning will be produced with which both producers and readers will agree.

The next chapter will examine the manner in which the advertisements *reinforced* this combination and, to some extent, remain an easily recognisable element of the past.

CHAPTER V

The Power of Advertising – War as a Metaphor:

"The War has already levied toll upon the complexion and caused wrinkles and lines to form where before was smooth skin. Left to fight its own battles, the skin will most surely succumb, but aided by Pomeroy Skin Food the face will come through the conflict scatheless..."

The proposal behind most of the advertising and articles, features and stories within the magazines was, and still is, that love in the shape of a man is the goal of every woman's life, and the only way to achieve that goal is by being physically and morally perfect. Women were, in most cases, a lot more financially dependent on men at this time; the magazines, to attract their readers, gave this dependence the romantic aura of love. Today, when this dependence has, in a much greater proportion, been removed, the underlying theme is still retained.

Advertisers continually made, and make, women aware of their alleged imperfections, then offer to sell them solutions through skin creams, shampoos, beauty hints, etc. The following are quotations from *Woman's Life* and *My Weekly*. They point to the continuing reinforcement of woman's needs:-

"Oriental Cream – the ideal, non-greasy toilet preparation used by Society and Professional women of two continents who are enthusiastic over the wonderful results obtainable." (July 1915).

"What can I put on my face to get rid of wrinkles? The short answer is nothing. Once wrinkles have formed, nothing you put on your face can make them go away again. However, moisturising will help to make them less apparent." (May 1989).

Readers were, and still are encouraged both by advertisers, and by the whole ethos of the magazines, to be perpetually anxious about whether they are wearing the right clothes, the right perfume.

Advertisers devise and exploit images of 'female identity', all of which seem to need satisfying by a whole range of products. The most pervasive image is still that of ideal mother and housewife, and is constantly perpetuated throughout the magazine, heavily favouring the twin themes of domesticity and sexual attractiveness. Marriage and the home are illustrated as women's pre-eminent social destiny, and the way they look, cook, clean and smell is what gets them there and keeps them there. Thus these stereotypes of femininity both separate women and endlessly reinforce their imperfections.

The image of 'woman' is that of an allegorical body – a perfect vessel, a container of fixed meanings – in contrast to an actual woman's imperfect and changing body. Both the contents and the advertising in the magazines constantly affirm the cult of femininity by continuing to suggest the female ability 'to lure, to delight – the power to persuade'.

The female form tends to be perceived in collective, universal and symbolic terms; the male as an individual, appearing to be in command of his own character and his own identity. The female form does not refer to particular women, unless as a recognisable symbol, such as the Virgin Mary or the Mona Lisa. The female form is used to sell every kind of consumer article. Her desirability, taken for granted, gives its light and energy to the product. Women are expected to identify with the subject in the image; men to experience desire through the image and then for the product the image represents. John Berger, in *Ways of Seeing*, suggests:-

> "... the essential way of seeing women, the essential use to which their images are put, has not changed. Women are depicted in a quite different way from men – not because the feminine is different from the masculine – but because the 'ideal' spectator is always assumed to be male and the image of the woman is designed to flatter him."

Women's magazines print pictures of women on their covers; so do men's; while experiments in male pin-ups appeal much less to women than vice versa. Where men often appear as themselves, as individuals, women endorse the identity and value of someone or something else, and the beholders' reactions are necessary to complete

their meaning – to desire the product the model, as 'woman', poses to sell.

By examining examples of advertising in the magazines before, during and after the First World War, it is possible to discover how the social changes and the upheavals of the war affected the approach to their readers in both overt and covert ways. Many of the advertisements were sufficiently well-established to be able to incorporate the war in their wording and graphics, in order to increase their impact. Others continued to offer bland, discreet solutions, backed up by 'references' and guarantees that followed the tone of the magazines' editorial features. The proportion of advertising to features and the fiction was considerably less than it is today, presumably because less funding was available and the companies advertising were smaller. Technological processes were not, obviously, so sophisticated. There was far less use of colour, and line drawing was used more than photography.

In spite of the outbreak of war and the changes in many women's lives, the advertisements consisted mainly of health remedies, white goods sales, domestic aids and food; just as they had done before the war (see *Woman's Life* of 1914, and *Home Chat* of 1915). *Tit Bits* of 1916 was very similar. Whether this was a deliberate policy or a fear of acceptance of change, consciously or unconsciously, is difficult to tell. The advertisements addressed the housewife, and were interspersed between the features and editorials. These, already, had a strongly overt war message, constantly exhorting their readers to economise and put all their energy into the war effort; yet, still appealing to the woman at home, the domestic consumer. *The Englishwoman* carried no advertisements; the readership addressed appears to have been the intellectual, politically aware 'new woman'. *Vogue*, in 1915, addressed their advertisements to the wealthy middle class reader of the magazine. Beautiful materials, a quality book shop, dental care in Harley Street. Here again, however, the war was a central part of the articles, but hardly mentioned in the advertisements, so the approach to the consumer was still on the basis of continuity of spending power.

In *Woman's Life*, 1918, there was a distinct change in the advertisements. New fabrics, perfume, an art course scholarship, chocolate as eaten by the troops, and an exhortation to buy war savings certificates, a stress on 'British Made' goods, all reached out

The Cocoa Girl

The Golden Age—the 'teens'—with all its buoyancy and spirit, is tempted to overdo physical effort. Stamina and a well-nourished frame are obtainable by regularly drinking FRY'S COCOA, so rich in vital elements. Before and after a game it is a wonderful "stay." Extolled by well-known people proficient in Sports and Pastimes.

Fry's

War's Anxieties.

The war will be responsible for many a premature line and wrinkle, and for deepening lines that have already begun to form. Many women are too occupied with war-thought to remember their appearance. The time is opportune, therefore, to remind them that a little forethought now will save much harm to the appearance later. Pomeroy Skin Food costs so little—only eighteenpence, in war as in peace—and it is so restful and healing to the "tired" complexion, that it is almost a duty to inculcate the use of it. Being British, there is no shortage of supply. The chemist and perfumer have it as usual. Gently worked into the face at bed-time, it feeds the skin-cells and keeps wrinkles at bay.—[ADVT.]

"'Here's a find,'

I thought to myself when
I first tested Rowntree's
Cocoa. I was feeling tired
after a long day in the yard,
but the cocoa soon put new
life into me. That was
weeks ago, and you'd think
the spell of it would wear
off after a time, *but I like it
more every time I taste it.*
As Dad says, 'It seems to
grow on one.' It's lucky
it's so inexpensive—I've
worked it out, and it costs
less than a halfpenny a
cup."

A Cup of
Rowntree's Cocoa

makes a biscuit into a meal

---

to a broader audience with more spending power. The advertisements were bolder, and used more space. By 1919, in *Home Chat*, the working woman began to appear in the advertisements:-

"I was feeling tired after a long day in the yard, but the cocoa soon put new life in to me."

"Women who have proved themselves capable of undertaking so much important work which was formerly done by men will not be slow to understand and avail themselves of any scheme for their benefit when it is plainly put before them."

Here are, therefore, with the beginning of mass market circulation, changes in the approach of the advertisements: less discreetly placed, more authoritative in their tone, attempting to reach the wider market of the working woman with more earning power and, hopefully, more spending power.

The war was often used as a metaphor in some of the advertisements. The actual events were taking place many miles away, but the advertisements drew on them in order to persuade women to fight their *own* war (*Woman's Life*, July 1915):-

"On many a woman's face today are traces of sleepless nights and anxious days. The war has already levied toll upon the complexion and caused wrinkles and lines to form where before was smooth skin. Left to fight its own battles, the skin will most surely succumb, but aided by Pomeroy Skin Food the face will come through the conflict scatheless... the preparation is British through and through."

Echoed in *My Weekly*, 1989, the battle here is, however, against the damaging effects of the sun:-

"As we know now that wrinkles are caused by over exposure to the sun, prevention means taking care to protect your skin, with a sunscreen, throughout summer."

The didactic approach of the editorials was rapidly echoed in the advertisements, and the messages they offered to the consumer were

105

equally as strong, from the publicity point of view. As their audience expanded rapidly, awareness of the opportunities to *create* need became a growing priority.

From the point of view of memory, it is very difficult to evaluate the long term effect. Although some of the women interviewed recognised the advertisements, there was more definite recognition of the fashions. For example, Rose, Molly and Susan all recognised the fashions of the time, and became involved in a lively conversation of memory about them. Rose also liked the 'weight reducing' advertisement and the article about 'women who should not be mothers'.

The impact of the advertisements seems, like the contents of the magazines, to have had a limited effect, an ephemeral impact. Unlike the sophisticated methods of constant repetition through magazines, newspapers, film and television advertising of today, there was a limited circulation and a less calculated and researched 'marketing' approach of the advertisers.

In the next chapter an examination will be made of the tacit understanding between producer and reader of the preferred fictional element of the magazines – and why this should be so.

CHAPTER VI

Escape into Fiction:

"We read the magazines to escape what was happening."

Pre-war magazines offered, through the serials and short stories, an escape to the glamorous life of mannequins in smart London stores, of nurses taken on long cruises by ailing employers, or aspiring actresses reaching the heights of stardom, a passport to a fantastic life as a working girl. However, the working girl during the war and in the post-war era, often in monotonous, badly paid employment, was offered via the magazines a world of cosy domesticity as well as an escape to a fantasy world.

In *Reading the Romance* Janice Rodway explores the assertion of various female readers that romance reading is a beneficial form of escape from the duties and responsibilities of domesticity; it provides much needed reassurance and, although this is probably questionable, helps them to learn about the outside world. The importance of a happy ending seems to lend credence to the general reliance on romantic fiction for its ability to raise the spirits of the reader. This requires involving the reader vicariously in the gradual evolution of a long relationship, whose culmination the reader is later permitted to enjoy through a description of the heroine's and hero's life together after their necessary union. This follows the 'working out' of the romance - the reinterpretation of misunderstood actions and eventual declarations of mutual love. *Woman's Life*, in September 1914, uses this format:-

"Violet Lumley was an English girl of the best type, high-spirited and warm-hearted, loving, upright, and courageous. Graham had never admitted to himself that women had any real part to play in the fortunes of the world. But, oddly enough, he never came into Violet Lumley's presence without longing to pour out to her all his thoughts and feelings."

"I had nothing to offer her before, and I have less than nothing now; I am lamed for life and my career is over."

107

"I knew that if I did not speak we should both lose the best that life has to give us. The worst of a woman's courage is that the world only blames her for it."

Implicitly, unhappiness and discord can be read from these stories as the consequence of insufficient love; the good relationship is the solution to every individual's problem. Thus the quintessential woman's magazine story has a plot structured around the pursuit of romantic love. Reproduced over and over again is the account of a peaceful initial period marred either by the breaking of social rules or misunderstanding or physical separation keeping hero and heroine apart, tests to be undergone before obstacles are finally surmounted, followed by the happy marriage. These are all *unchanging elements* of the magazines. They still recur in both the magazines and in romantic fiction, such as the Mills and Boon romances; today endorsed and enjoyed, also, in both film and television drama. Many of the plots revolve around a transcendence by the heroine of the boundaries of wealth and social class – the 'chorus girl married to the duke' variety; for example, in *My Weekly* of January 1916 – 'Queen of the Stage; or The Mill girl Star'. Following in the footsteps of the mythological elements of fairy tales, or the 'lost and found' stories that Shakespeare drew on, the heroine may emerge as ultimately not to be true working class; a hero may be cut off from his wealthy background and forced to live a 'working class' existence, as shown in *My Weekly*, January 1916:-

"But it was not until the day when Zoe, radiantly happy and looking lovelier than she had ever looked before, stood at Jim's side as his bride, that she learned the secret of his birth. As he drew her close Jim told her of all that Mr Markham had discovered, proving that he, Jim, was the rightful owner of the Hall..."

Thus in social origin the hero and heroine may ultimately turn out to be alike, although the main theme of the story has concerned the proving of their fitness to marry each other. Again, an unexpected inheritance may alter the total dependence of the lower class heroine on the upper class hero – as in *Jane Eyre* by Charlotte Brontë.

There is some recognition in the magazine plots of changes within British society, including such areas of discussion as going out to work or remaining at home, the decline of tradition and the growth of the importance of friendship over blood ties. Yet there remains the dependence of the story writers on and, presumably, acceptance by their readers of, dominant middle class values.

The importance of work emerges with overwhelming clarity throughout the magazine stories. Work is considered intrinsically valuable, and not merely tied to other values such as wealth. Descriptions of heroes typically include some reference to commitment to work, as though this were a necessary element of fitness for the heroic role. In the magazines of wartime, soldiering is seen as the paramount task of almost every hero. In *Tit Bits*, January, 1916, the hero is a classic example:-

> "There followed for Alan a few months of training, and then the great business of war began. With that business we have little to do. Where brave men are gathered, brave deeds will always be done, and one of the bravest deeds of all fell to the share of Alan Chesney... When he was at length well enough to return to England, he was informed that he would be unfit for further service. Well, he was satisfied. He had done his bit, and he could do no more."

Following convention, the men were all shown to be brave or heroic – there is no mention of men expressing their fear. The war literature, discussed in Chapter VIII, tells quite a different story.

It is interesting to follow the course of the 'soldier/hero' in the magazines during and after the war. In *Home Chat* of September 1914, the hero is a soldier in India, indicating the shape of things to come. He is a volunteer. The heroes of the other serials are still either doctors or businessmen. In 1916, the heroes of the stories are still part of life in England, one being a doctor again. The heroine's father in one of the serials is a source of problems to his daughter, as the fact that he is in 'trade' makes her life at boarding school very difficult. Snobbishness is still a very strong element; again, a 'middle class' value for a 'working class' reader. In *Woman's Life*, 1915, one hero is a rich baronet, the other a captain in the army. A change in the hero was gradually beginning to emerge, but the main changes seemed to appear *after* the war. This more slowly changing attitude towards the hero in magazine fiction than that of actual social change, is an example of the gap between the continuous pattern of magazine production and the rapid change of circumstances of the reader.

In *Home Chat* of 1919 the heroine is a WREN and the hero is an *American* soldier, although his use of language is a very mixed bag of English and American phrases such as a 'topping' house, and 'Waal, I guess'. The other stories have an airman as hero, a traitor in the pay of the German government as the villain, and, in the final story, a tall man with a limp and '3 little stripes of gold on his civilian cuffs'. In *My Weekly* of 1918 the hero saves a deserter and takes him back to the Front as his batman. There is no question about 'going back'. In *Woman's Life* of 1918 the hero has a mysterious 'past'. He has not served in the war, as he has been out of the country. In another story, the heroine works in an aeroplane factory. The hero has a limp and a VC.

Any sign of disenchantment with the conditions and wages of the working class is carefully eliminated. Unemployment is always seen as the product of fate, beyond human control; yet contradictory to this is the assumption that only the morally inadequate fail to find work. At the same time, the stories portray success as often being due to good luck as well as hard-earned achievement.

It is where content offers itself as being instantly recognisable to every strata of society - as in these romantic stories - that dominant middle class values are least successfully concealed. The stories are not simply a neutral window on a diverse world, but express a particular way of *seeing the world*. It is possible to detect an underlying unity based upon a partial and selective mode of seeing the world and representing it to the reader. Events are portrayed in terms of the actions and interactions of individuals, strongly governed by luck, fate and chance within a *given* naturalised world, which appears to form an unchanging background. This is a diverse panorama of individuals reunited in the form of a community that shares common universal experiences: birth, love, death, accident, illness and, in the period under discussion, war; as well as, crucially, the common experience of consuming. This community is further given focus by the stock of common sense assumptions about the world implicit in this type of human interest story. Identification is also invited with symbols of national unity, who are presented as being above narrow

MISS GERTIE MILLAR, ALWAYS VERY NEAR TO THE HEART

OF THE LONDON PUBLIC, RETURNS TO SCORE NEW TRIUMPHS

IN "HOUP-LA," MR. CHARLES B. COCHRAN'S DELIGHT-

FULLY GOWNED PRODUCTION AT THE NEW ST. MARTIN'S

Affection for Miss Gertie Millar is almost a national tradition, and this is not surprising, since this charming artist has only to appear on the stage to infect her audience with her own indomitable joie de vivre. She seems to be enjoying herself so thoroughly, to find life so entertaining, and the particular play of the moment such remarkably good fun, that in spite of oneself one is carried away. She has lately returned from America, and is now the bright particular star of "Houp-La," where as Tillie Runstead, leading equestrienne in her uncle's circus, she infatuates Peter Carey, polo-player and millionaire, to the extent of making him work for a living as a groom in the circus for two pounds a week. Her song, "The Fool of the Family," is the success of the evening, and the quaint and delightful costume in which she sings it might have been inspired by Aubrey Beardsley

political differences. The stories represent the world of experience, the world of individuals, as opposed to the impersonal, 'ivory tower' mentality of institutions.

Audience identification with these personal dramas is, therefore, constructed around universal and eternal elements of experience. Its whole process of individualised presentation, portrayal of events from a human interest standpoint and the generation of symbols of national identity, can be illustrated by reference to the portrayal of celebrities, as in *Vogue* of 1916:-

> "Affection for Miss Gertie Millar is almost a national tradition, and this is not surprising, since this charming artist has only to appear on the stage to infect her audience with her own indomitable joie de vivre. She seems to be enjoying herself so thoroughly, to find life so entertaining, and the particular play of the moment such remarkably good fun, that in spite of oneself one is carried away."

Their private lives become the focus of interest; while remaining glamorous, they are also seen as 'just like us', offering a unity based on the concept of happiness linked to consumption. In the same way, the 'hero' is shown as being only *just* out of reach of the reader's fantasy – the boss, the doctor, the heir to considerable wealth. He is never in a profession *totally* unattainable; always just out of reach, like the consumer goods advertised in the magazines. Social mobility through entertainment or artistic success is also shown as important, depending upon innate talent rather than the promise of reward through work. The tendency here is to present success as a reward for virtue – the approved characters are given opportunities through work, education or discovery. The underlying image of society which is presented is, therefore, one in which escape and success, aspiration and ambition, are seen in terms of the personal and arbitrary on the one hand, and the reward reaped by a sacrificial acceptance of the work ethic on the other. Society is shown as static and fixed, except for these lucky individuals.

The apparent sense of an underlying unity between classes is sustained by presentation of the rich in the domestic sphere. Class relationships rarely appear in work settings, thus tending to conceal structural inequality and to smooth over the sense of deprivation or powerlessness which might be felt by working class readers. Wealth is also portrayed as a 'decorative trimming' as the stories focus on ritualised, glamorous occasions, and on the acquisition of material possessions (*Woman's Life*, December 1918):-

> "...they went out into the wide, panelled hall, where a log fire burned on the open hearth, and huge vases of late roses and chrysanthemums gave out a pleasant scent. There was an air of comfort and ease about, the calm security that wealth long held gives..."

However there is an *implied* social difference for those less approved characters:-

> "... that filled Zoe's heart with envy. Gwen was mistress of the charming house, of the large income that went with it, whilst Zoe was only a dependent, and when Gwen got married her reason for existing would be gone."

Yet it is implied that the same everyday experiences of life and the same values or interests run parallel with those of the reader, unless the characters are those of whom the reader is expected to disapprove. Money is perceived as an *individual* reward for merit and status, and in this respect the magazine stories continue to reflect the hopes of the 'industrial' novelists of the 1840s: that ultimately the rich and poor can inhabit the same world.

The romantic love ethos of these stories is carefully distinguished from any depiction of passionate love or eroticism, and is based on the attraction of the whole personality, not on physical ties. At the same time, the heroines appear to have no personality: they are pretty, unobtrusive adornments to every day life. The largest number of heroes are businessmen or doctors or soldiers, the 'chivalrous knight' who must pass various tests before being rewarded with romantic marriage. They are people whom the 'working girl' reader might meet, but have very little chance of marrying. The stories show commitment to professional rules rather than to emotions.

Another consistent element in the structure of these stories, which reinforces their interpretation as modern myth, is the association of the country with purity, and the city with constraint and artificiality.

113

There is, therefore, a paradox that in magazines circulating extensively amongst an urban working class the advanced industrial society is symbolically ignored. Urban life is seen as fundamentally restless, atomised and mechanistic, and country life becomes the focus of moral sentiment and understanding, as in *Woman's Life*, December 1918:-

> "To the petted and cherished girl, who all her life had been guarded from rough contact with the realities of life, it was a horrible sensation to realise that she was alone in London without money. She had no idea as to what she should do, she could think of no one to whom she could apply for help... Gwen was so ignorant of the ways and manners of the majority of landladies that she did not realise with what distinction she was being treated... she drank the tea eagerly, and then ate a little of the greyish-looking bread and butter... Hollows and the gloriously happy life that had been hers seemed so far away."

The magazine fiction, therefore, continues to use a convention that has its roots in the major literary tradition of Dickens, Eliot and Gaskell, for example, which is seen as using rural idealisation to 'attempt to reconcile some conflict between the parts of society and to reconcile the conflicts of an individual in whom those of society will be mirrored.' This is discussed by Bridget Fowler in *Popular Fiction and Social Change*. Signs of such idealisation in these stories are that moments of harmony – declarations of love, endings, etc. – tend to take place in the country, and that 'valued' characters are countrymen or have their social roots in the country (as seen in *My Weekly*, August 1918):-

> "He was a cheery old man, and with a merry twinkle in his keen blue eyes told us to jump up. Quickly we scrambled up on top of the sweet, fragrant-smelling hay, and rumbled along the country road, happy monarchs of all we surveyed... the rear lights of the train disappeared round the curve, leaving me alone with my memories of a day fragrant with sweet thoughts of love and happiness."

LETTER IV.

DEAREST Eileen,

To-day is glorious:

"The little birds sang east,
and the little birds sang west."

At dawn they were carolling in the sunshine. The may was opening; at noon it was blossoming.

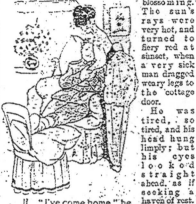

The sun's rays were very hot, and turned to fiery red at sunset, when a very sick man dragged weary legs to the cottage door.

He was tired, so tired, and his head hung limply; but his eyes looked straight ahead, as if seeking a haven of rest. He walked with the aid of a stick, for one leg was straight and stiff.

"I've come home," he said, opening his tired eyes.

For a moment it seemed my heart stopped beating—the world was upside-down. A chaos of feeling brought my tears, and then laughter, and finally tears and laughter together.

ISN'T IT FUNNY THE WAY TWO PEOPLE — THE STOLID BRITISH PEOPLE, I MEAN—WILL MEET AFTER A LONG ABSENCE?

It seems that a natural instinct restrains the first rush of words, and curbs the impulse that love and happiness would make.

"Hallo!" said I, drawling the first syllable of that silly word, and bringing, or trying to bring, a wealth of welcome into the "o."

"How are you, billet girl?"

He was almost dead with the long walk, and so weak that I had to lead him to an armchair—his armchair—and pile the cushions behind his head, and rest his poor, shattered leg on a cradle of them.

"I've come home," he said, opening his tired eyes.

"Yes, dear?"

"Put your arms round my neck!

Tighter—tighter! Yes, like that! my dear, there is a Heaven, after all.

Then I think he slept. How long I do not know, for I was kneeling beside his chair, my arms round him, his head pillowed on my shoulder. And there is no count of time in Heaven!

Afterwards, he said:

"I used to dream of this out there. When things were quiet in the trenches, and we lay hour after hour, I would picture a little chintz room, and a little girl with the firelight making ruddy lights in her hair; and I used to wonder how she would welcome me when I went back, if she would have another soldier in my place, or if she would be just alone as I first saw her.

"And as I lay wounded down at the base hospital, I used to write to her, telling of all the things I would have said before I went away!"

"Why didn't you say them? Why didn't you send the letters? Oh, you idiot of a man, you dear, dear silly! Why didn't you send them? What hours of anxiety and gallons of tears you would have saved!"

"Tears! Were they for me? Did you care? Do you care? Little girl, I'm only a crock now, lame and useless, and I'm a cad to ask you such a thing!"—

"You are the dearest crock I ever knew, and as for——"

But his kisses sealed my lips.

OH, I AM HAPPY, HAPPY, HAPPY!

Good-bye.

115

For the writers, the function of country life is to serve as an escape from the consequences of urban capitalism. For the reader, the resolution of conflict taking place in a pastoral rather than an urban setting helps to reiterate the rural myth and constantly assuage the psychological need for escape into a fantasy world. The rural idyll of cottage/home, too, has a strong identification in 'popular' ideology with the woman as symbol of peace and quiet, and the 'wholeness' of the organic community (*Home Chat*, July 1915):-

> "The may was opening; at noon it was blossoming...
> When things were quiet in the trenches, and we lay hour
> after hour, I would picture a little chintz room, and a little
> girl, with the firelight making ruddy lights in her hair... I
> weep, but my tears fall in that merciful darkness called
> night, and I am brave in the day and work to forget, as
> women do."

The continuing structure of the magazine story is, therefore, one of possessive individualism, divided into two alternative images: firstly, that the deserving are rewarded by magical good fortune and, secondly, that an organic social order can only be seen in terms of the pastoral. The nature of the plots must contain the consequences for individuals of the experiences of poverty, wage labour and injury to social standing. The images of women are drawn within the valued ideals of domesticity, self-effacement and altruism, even though the demands of realism draw out doubts, dissatisfactions and minor rebellions against the domestic role. While produced for a mainly working class readership, the stories are, therefore, underpinned by the dominant ideology of the middle class, even though the particular combination of patterns is historically variable.

One of the major aims of magazine proprietors is to produce magazines in forms which they regard as pleasurable commodities with which women are able to relax. By doing so, they have a tendency to represent women's lives as *only* pleasurable, satisfying and enjoyable. Yet this is obviously not true for many women – as the problem pages show. It is, therefore, possible to suggest that in providing pleasure in a particular way they do, perhaps, exploit a suggestion that women's lives are contented and easy. The dominant mechanisms of pleasure relate both to the process of identification – of

116

women seeing themselves both as they are and as they might become – and the process of escape into a world which is not their own. The production of pleasure by a text and the notion of social reading suggests how the reader is actively involved in the process of reading. The magazine, through its verbal and visual representations, generates pleasure and, simultaneously, recognition and effect, as discussed in *The Changing Experience of Women*:-

> "Reality is not what magazines stories have been for. They provide women with a world which is larger than life, more romantic, more exciting, more ordered than their own world. They want to lose themselves in it for the moment and then come back satisfied, to their own familiar lives."

In particular, women's magazine stories are not just about fantasy. Their background is the 'ordinariness' of personal relations in everyday life, approached through the fictional form. They deal explicitly with the everyday, but not the changing tensions and struggles for femininity for women. Just as the advertisements deal with the reinforcement of that femininity – the outcome of the struggle – the stories provide not only fictional representations of the problems of personal experience, but also fictional solutions. There is a 'woman's' narrative in the representations which begins in girlhood and moves on to marriage and motherhood. There are some features about childhood, rarely any about old age, and they 'peak' around relationships with men, of which there are endless variations. If paid work for women makes an appearance, it is a peripheral concern to relationships. Rarely does friendship between women figure in the narratives. The representation of women is stereotyped, and the plots detail clichéd feminine and masculine behaviour. They tend to have marked narrative resolutions, invariably hopeful and optimistic. The stories and features reaffirm a pattern, even in times of social change, of traditional femininity and of a traditional division of labour between wife and husband, very noticeable in the period under discussion; with wife as primarily housekeeper and mother, seeking satisfaction within those roles, and husband as primarily breadwinner, and sole sexual and emotional provider for his wife.

The most enjoyable part of romance reading, the true escape, is the opportunity to project oneself into the story; to *become* the heroine, and thus to share her surprise and slowly awakening pleasure at being so closely watched by someone who finds her valuable. *My Weekly*, January, 1916, has a good example:-

> "That longed for moment when at last, no barriers resting between them, Zoe and Jim stood face to face, seemed too sacred for spoken words. His glowing, love filled eyes burned into hers, and slowly he stretched out his arms towards her. 'At last, Zoe! I have wanted you so!'... Like a tired child she nestled in the shelter of his arms."

Because the reader experiences the pleasure vicariously, her own need for a caring, nurturing relationship is assuaged only as long as she can displace it on to a fictional character. When that character's story is completed, when the serial or story in the magazine is finished, the reader is forced to return to herself and her real situation. Therefore, the fiction's short-lived, therapeutic value is finally the cause of its repetitive consumption.

Providing relaxing domestic entertainment offers apparently readily acceptable values at the level of fantasy, rather than concrete reality; a world of at once known and familiar territory and a region of tranquil escape. Yet this continuing escape is able, temporarily, to remove their women readers from the psychologically demanding and emotionally draining task of attending to the physical and affective needs of their families - a task that is particularly theirs. Socially conditioned to believe that women are especially and naturally attuned to the emotional requirements of others, they still value reading this type of fiction because it is an *intensely private act*. It also enables them to suspend temporarily familial relations and to place themselves apart from the need constantly to relate to others.

It is also *compensatory* literature. It supplies them with an important emotional release which is not possible in daily life, because the social role with which they identify themselves leaves little room for guiltless, self-interested pursuit of individual pleasure.

Romance reading might be seen, therefore, as a collectively elaborated female ritual - as is the 'cult' of femininity itself - through which women explore the consequences of their common social condition - the magazines are both able and determined to provide this - and attempt to imagine a more perfect state where all the needs they so intensely feel and accept as given would be adequately rewarded. However, although romance writing and reading help to create a kind of female community the activity may, in fact, remove the need or desire to demand satisfaction in the real world because it can be successfully met in fantasy. It would certainly appear from examination of a current magazine that enjoyment of romantic stories is a *continuing* process, not only from the point of view of this need for compensatory literature, but because recognition of an area in the magazine which is always there, and always expected to be there, brings a sense of security in a changing world. Certainly those witnesses who had read the magazines over the years were invariably pleased to recognise a familiar area within them (*My Weekly*, May 1989):-

> "Clive Redmond was special and, for a change, a man was besotted with me. He was so attentive that I went around on a cloud of happiness. This was it, I told myself, and saw the future all mapped out. My tall, dark-haired, wonderful man had said he loved me. The next step was obviously marriage."

The seamless, repetitive quality of this fiction, with its carefully comfortable images, contains nothing of the wartime propaganda element of the editorial features and advertising in the other sections of the magazines, as we have already seen.

In the next chapter we examine the emotional blackmail of many of the images used, both in the magazines and in the posters which appeared at the time. The use of propaganda is strongly echoed in the attitudes of wartime and, again, in the reality of women's capabilities when given the opportunity to serve. Included are details of the active work of the land army girls, the munitions workers and those who worked as VADs.

CHAPTER VII

Emotional Blackmail:

"Is your 'Best Boy' wearing Khaki? If not, don't you think he should be? If he does not think that you and your country are worth fighting for – do you think he is WORTHY of you?"

6th August, 1914:

"If I am asked what we are fighting for..." said the Prime Minister in the House of Commons, "...I can reply in two sentences. In the first place to fulfil a solemn international obligation – an obligation which, if it had been entered into between private persons in the ordinary concerns of life, would have been regarded as an obligation not only of law, but of honour, which no self-respecting man could possibly have repudiated."

"I say, secondly, we are fighting to vindicate the principle... that small nationalities are not to be crushed, in defiance of international good faith, by the arbitrary will of a strong and overmastering Power."

"I do not believe any nation ever entered into a great controversy... with a clearer conscience and strong conviction that it is fighting... in defence of principles the maintenance of which is vital to the civilisation of the world..."

This consciousness-raising attitude filtered down and was absorbed not only by adults, but also by children in school. Dorothy was very proud of the letter shown below, which was published in the *Selby Times*:-

"At ten years of age at school, we had to write to the Kaiser as a composition. 'It is beneath me to write to you at all, but as I have to do it I will make the best of it. How is your son the Crown Prince? We call him the Clown Prince. I hope (?) will change their minds and go with the Old Firm. Yours in disgust, an English schoolgirl.'"

Photo. *Hoffmann & Bu...*

The German Emperor a
Count von Wedel, Statthal
of Alsace-Lorraine.

As propaganda to increase involvement in the war effort got under way in 1914 women were addressed specifically in their own magazines and in posters designed to support the recruitment drive. Women's new role demanded a new image. Magazines, posters, films and paintings depicted the new desirable stereotype. She was 'the girl behind the man behind the gun', the munitionette, the VAD or the Land Girl. British posters showed women engaged in industrial and agricultural production for the war effort. Other familiar figures in the war posters were the women in the home – 'Women of Britain Say Go' is the clear message. Other posters depicted woman as the mother, not wasting bread – the flour for which sailors have risked their lives to import – or in prayer with her tiny child: 'God bless dear Daddy who is fighting the Hun and send him Help'.

Dorothy was not so proud, however, of the effect of her desire to help the war effort on other people:-

"I used to sing with other children from my school in village halls at meetings for young men to volunteer. I used to sing solo. One particular evening I sang 'Oh we don't want to lose you, but we think you ought to go'. One young man stood up and said, 'I'll make one.' He enlisted and was killed within one week. I was very upset, and felt responsible. I still do. I put everything into my singing."

The 'young women of London' were asked:-

"Is your 'Best Boy' wearing Khaki? If not, don't you think he should be? If he does not think that you and your country are worth fighting for – do you think he is WORTHY of you?... Think it over – then ask him to JOIN THE ARMY TODAY."

This poster's simplified arguments and use of emotional blackmail are typical of the crude, but effective, fusion of personal and idealistic motives that formed the basis of the appeal to women.

A copy of *Home Chat* of 1915 suggests that class barriers should be removed in wartime for the common good, and uses this pre-war article as a basis for propaganda:-

"NATIONAL SERVICE and why I believe it would do the average boy a world of good... I know its advantages, which are tremendous – and its drawbacks, which are certainly worth considering, but slight in comparison... The men around you, many of them, are not the class of men you are accustomed to mix with, and you do not enjoy their society at all... And then, somewhere about the end of the first week, an extraordinary thing happens. You blush with shame when you remember how you looked down on your companions. Rough they may be, but you have learnt what fine, sporting, generous fellows they are, for nothing shows up a man's real soul like life in camp... And that is why I believe that compulsory soldiering will do more good to the young men of our country than anything else under the sun."

When war did begin, this type of propaganda for recruitment was reinforced by the use of posters like the famous one of Lord Kitchener and when the British Expeditionary Force left for France on the 17th August, 1914, it helped to strengthen the Prime Minister's message earlier in the month. Before leaving, every soldier received this message from the King:-

"You are leaving home to fight for the safety and honour of my Empire. Belgium, whose country we are pledged to defend, has been attacked, and France is about to be invaded by the same powerful foe. I have implicit confidence in you, my soldiers. Duty is your watchword, and I know your duty will be nobly done. I shall follow your every movement with deepest interest and mark with eager satisfaction your daily progress; indeed, your welfare will never be absent from my thoughts."

"I pray God to bless you and guard you, and bring you back victorious."

Good advice was also given by Lord Kitchener:-

"Be invariably courteous, considerate and kind. Never do anything likely to injure or destroy property, and always

Lord Kitchener,
British War Minister.

"We are coming, brothers, coming,
A hundred thousand strong!"

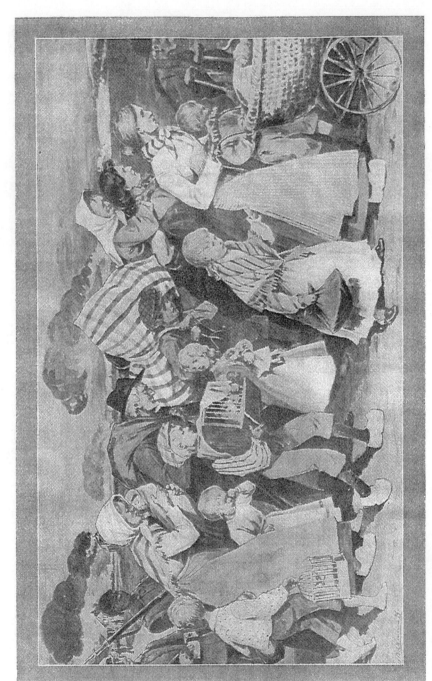

From painting by Jan Wiegman.

Belgian Refugees.

BRAVO, BELGIUM!

(*By permission of the Proprietors of "Punch."*)

THE TRIUMPH OF "CULTURE."

(By permission of the Proprietors of "PUNCH.")

133

Effect of German "Kultur" at Termonde and Louvain.

THE DAILY MIRROR

"THREE CHEERS

FOR BELGIUM!"

look upon looting as a disgraceful act. You are sure to meet with a welcome and to be trusted; your conduct must justify that welcome and that trust... Keep consistently upon your guard against any excesses... Do your duty bravely. Fear God. Honour the King."

The irony implicit in these instructions was to become obvious more swiftly than anyone could have realised.

The alleged behaviour of German soldiers in Belgium gave rise to expressions of outrage in the British press. Again, the posters used this 'news' to bolster recruitment:-

REMEMBER BELGIUM. OFFER YOUR SERVICES NOW. THERE'S STILL A PLACE IN THE LINE FOR YOU. IF YOU CANNOT JOIN THE ARMY TRY AND GET A RECRUIT.

Even *The Englishwoman*, a sober and more politically aware magazine, was emotionally aroused to join in the general outcry against the 'unspeakable barbarities of German soldiers'. By November 1914 *The Englishwoman*'s brand of chauvinism was beginning to evolve:-

"War is brutal, barbarous, materialistic, whereas women's influence in the world is of the spirit."

Yet, the article continues:-

"...this war is really a war on our part for the maintenance of moral principle as against brute force."

Thus it was condoning the 'brutality' of war as a moral principle not opposed to women's 'spirit'. In an edition of November 1915 also, acceptance of a report on the conditions of German prisoner of war camps in Britain offers a reiteration of this element of partiality:-

"'In almost every case,' the inspector remarks, 'there is no criticism to be made of this camp.' The complaints of prisoners are almost always the same, requests for

German prisoners of war in England. Above, senior German officers at Holyport Camp, Maidenhead [*photo source: R. C. W. Hill*]; left, a view of the camp at Frongach, Wales, in wintry conditions. [*Photo source: Mrs V. M. M. White*]

(1) German Prisoners in Antwerp.
(2) Concentration Camp for Prisoners at Camberley.

repatriation, requests for liberty to take walks in the country... they have every facility for amusing themselves. The death rate is very low. In one camp, where 4000 men were interned, they had had twelve deaths in eighteen months, but since three of these occurred within a few days the prisoners 'were nervous about the hospital treatment'. We cannot, it is to be feared, expect this unimpeachable record will have any effect in inducing the German authorities to treat their prisoners with more humanity, but it is a statement of which we have a right to be proud."

It was felt, too, that a girl's moral standards could be deduced from her taste in dress, and a strong propagandist element was shown in condemnation of the 'craze for extravagant and even ridiculous underwear' in the magazines. Here is an example from *My Weekly* of January, 1916:-

"As an example of the sort of thing that can only be called a national disgrace when indulged in at a time like this, I recently saw knickers, chemises, night-dresses and combinations of pale blue georgette, exquisitely hand-embroidered..."

Vogue's wartime function, however, was to promote austerity and self-restraint, as in other magazines of the period, but to provide an antidote to the general depression and the impoverishment of living standards:-

"Nervous people do well to avoid this number; it is full of thrilling surprises in costumes and hair-raising adventures in millinery, and its short stories about lingerie are apt to be just the least bit risqué."

"Christmas will hardly be gay this year, but the young people must be catered for, and informal festivities, therefore, will be the order of the day. The consciousness of being unsuitably dressed paralyses one's conversation, and makes one an unutterably dull guest. In common

fairness to our host we should go so clad as to be unaware
of our clothes."

"Propaganda is active in favour of economy. We are
urged to spend money on necessities, not luxuries. Good!
But between Economy and Philanthropy there must be
l'entente cordiale."

By November 1918 *Vogue* was expressing, for its readers, a tone
of regret that their part in the war effort had come to an end:-

"For many women the end of the war must necessarily
imply the closing of a stimulating chapter of experiences...
Many a chauffeuse in navy blue or military khaki will regret
the Mercedes in which she came to have almost a
proprietary interest."

At the end of the war it was agreed that women on the whole had
shown up well in the course of it; now they were thanked, suitably
rewarded with the vote – if they were over thirty – and sent home.
Public opinion assumed that all women could still be supported by
men and that, if they went on working, it was from a sort of
deliberate wickedness. The tone of the press swung, all in a moment,
from extravagant praise to the opposite extreme, and the very same
people who had been heroines and saviours of their country a few
months before were now parasites, blacklegs and limpets. Employers
were implored to turn them out as passionately as they had been
exhorted to employ them.

Yet pre-war ideas about women's limited capacities had been
forcibly modified. This might have led to adjustments in the national
approach to job distribution and training schemes – but it did not. The
official approach had not been to consider the true capabilities of
women; rather it was that publicising the success of women as
substitutes for male workers might persuade more employers to
release more men for active service. It was continually emphasised
that whatever was learnt – by women, men, employers, workers or
government – during the war about women's roles as workers was to
be confined to the war period. All that women were allowed to think
they had proved was their ability to temporarily substitute for men.

Persuasion to make women relinquish ideas of independence and sexual equality was widely used. (Discussed in examination of women's magazines in *Women and Children First*, by Mary Cadogen and Patricia Gray):-

"To many – especially women – the war has brought responsibility and conspicuous service of which peace must necessarily deprive them."

Vogue (also mentioned in their book) was, however, sufficiently affected by current pressures to shirk effective consideration of the issue:-

"There are few who would not rather have the men than the men's jobs".

This implied a kind of inborn right; and women's sexuality and femininity were put forward as an alternative to a more independent way of life. Other magazines took up the chorus:-

"The tide of progress which leaves woman with the vote in her hand and scarcely any clothes on her back is ebbing, and the sex is returning to the deep, very deep sea of femininity from which her newly-acquired power can be more effectively wielded."

The Englishwoman, however, tried to combat these pressures with a very strong article on the need to consider women's future place in industry:-

"In itself, this problem, which calls on the best brains of the country for its solution, and is also worthy of close and sympathetic consideration by all ranks in the great army of industry, is no novelty. It must be worthy of the services they have rendered their country in the hour of its greatest need... They themselves would be the last to expect or even to desire that the mobilised men whose places they filled should not be reinstated upon their return... But... they demand that they should have a fair field, rightly considering that their continued employment in industries in which they have gained valuable experience... should not be regarded as a favour."

Many women war workers had been affected as much as men by unambiguous patriotism; some were no more immune from propaganda than their menfolk. For the young women who had faced no prospect but enforced boredom in provincial towns and villages, the sudden encouragement to leave home and find adventure and excitement at the Front, or in jobs they had never thought to do before, had as exhilarating an effect as it had for the young men.

Many men and boys returning to civilian life from the forces found it impossible to get work. By 1920 more than four million men had been released from the services. Reabsorption of most of them into civil employment was made possible not only by the economic boom of 1919, but by discharging the women from jobs in industry to make way for these ex-servicemen. Some of their bitterness was directed against the new independent, wage-earning women whose numbers had increased dramatically since pre-1914 days – even though many of these women had to earn their own living for they had few opportunities of finding husbands to support them. Circumstances denied them the traditional role of wife and mother, yet they were illogically expected to forgo their right to work. Several newspapers went so far as to exhort emigration. Thus, after the war, many women were forced to give back their jobs to returning war heroes and go back to housework.

Yet the women had taken on jobs they had never dreamt previously of doing, and demonstrated the scope of their ability to the world and also surprised themselves. The argument that women were physically and mentally only capable of acting as helpmeets to men was firmly dislodged.

If we look at some details of the working lives of, for example, the VADs, the munitionettes and the land army recruits, this capability and strength will be all too easily proven, particularly in view of the extremely arduous routine of their working lives.

Lynn Macdonald describes the VAD (a member of the Voluntary Aid Detachment) in her book *The Roses of No Man's Land*, as follows:-

Girls of the Forestry
Department, Land Army,
Basildon Park. [*Photo source:
Colonel E. G. Galley*]

Enrolment of Land Army girls, c. 1915-16.
A photograph taken at Mr J. Thisleton-Smith's farm at West Barsham, Norfolk.
Miss Burton-Fanning presents an armband to a cook/dairymaid.

"She is called Elsie or Gladys or Dorothy. Her ankles are swollen, her feet are aching, her hands reddened or rough. She has little money, no vote, and has almost forgotten what it feels like to be really warm. She sleeps in a tent. Unless she has told a diplomatic lie about her age, she is twenty-three. She is the daughter of a clergyman, a lawyer or a prosperous businessman, and has been privately educated and groomed to be a 'lady'. She wears the unbecoming outdoor uniform of a VAD or an army nurse. She is on active service, and as much a part of the war as 'Tommy Atkins'."

Vera Brittain, in her book *Testament of Youth*, gives her description of her life as a VAD:-

"We went on duty at 7.30 a.m. and came off at 8 p.m. Our hours, including three hours' off-time and a weekly half day – all of which we gave up willingly enough whenever a convoy came in or the ward was full of unusually bad cases – thus amounted to a daily twelve and a half. We were never allowed to sit down in the wards, and our off-duty time was seldom allocated before the actual day. Night duty, from 8 p.m. to 8 a.m. over a period of two months, involved a twelve hour stretch without off-time, though one night's break was usually allowed in the middle. For this work we received the magnificent sum of £20 a year, plus a tiny uniform allowance and the cost of our laundry."

She goes on to describe her feelings when, after the Battle of the Somme (July 1916), the huge convoys came through "without cessation for about a fortnight, and continued at short intervals for the whole of that sultry month and the first part of August. Day after day I had to fight the queer, frightening sensation of seeing the covered stretchers come in, one after another, without knowing until I ran with pounding heart to look what fearful sight or sound or stench, what problem of agony or imminent death, each brown blanket concealed."

Carol Twinch, in *Women on the Land*, describes the lives of the land army recruits:-

"At the height of the war the Land Army had a full time membership of 23,000 members. With the coming of the war, thousands of women from comparatively ordinary backgrounds were suddenly required to go far beyond the old boundaries of dairying and gardening into a hitherto male-dominated world of heavy horses, ploughing and field work. Women unused to labouring, or even to country life, were called upon to help maintain vital food supplies for the nation. Hundreds of untrained women were to venture further, to work in the woods and forests, felling timber to provide pit props for the mines, as well as working in the huge and dangerous sawmills."

"The conditions under which the women volunteers lived and worked were often far removed from those to which they were used, and they had also to contend with resentful male farm workers who viewed them as 'blackleg' labour. The farmers were unprepared and angry, when their skilled men were recruited for war service, and indignant when told that the Government proposed to increase the number of women volunteers being sent on to the land, and that women were to be virtually the only new source of labour. However, the pride which the women took in their achievements has shone through, and some to this day have retained a close affinity for farming. It is clear that for many those years opened up an entirely new way of life; an opportunity to do something completely out of the run of their normal lives. For some it represented a time of growing up, and of acquiring the self-confidence to cope with the tough realities of the world in which they found themselves; for others their time on the land simply offered adventure."

One of the women interviewed for this book (Doris) talked about her life on the land in these terms:-

"I worked on a farm during the war. I learnt a lot of things. Previously I did not know a cow from a bull! I learnt to calve a cow, ring pigs and ride a horse. I was then

143

LAND OUTFITS, OVERALLS, BLOUSES, Etc.

HEALTH BELT.

SPECIAL ATTENTION is directed to our Health Belt, made for land workers and all women in outdoor occupations. This Body Belt is made in soft natural flannel, much care having been given to the shape and design, and it will be found absolutely comfortable and easy in wear. This Belt protects the wearer from Chills, Rheumatism and kindred ailments. Waist measure only required. Price 7/6 each.

THE "STANDARD" OUTFIT.

HAT.
Stitched brim, lined, close fitting, shady.
3/11

COMPLETE OUTFIT
35/-

SHIRT.
Well made and well cut. Buttons at wrist.
6/11

BREECHES.
Tailor effect, laced-up knees, buttons at hips, straps and buckles at waist. Can be worn with or without Coat.
10/11

PUTTEES.
Standard size. Army pattern. Full length, cut on bias, long tapes to fasten.
2/11

Sizes: SMALL, MEDIUM, LARGE.

THE "COAT SMOCK" is a very smart Farm Overall with a tailor-made effect. It can be worn with the Standard Outfit. In Amazon 11/9, Mercerised Casement 12/11, Plaid Zephyr 13/11, Khaki Jean 13/11, Munition Brown Jean 14/11.

THE "IDEAL" HAT.

For Landworkers and others. Very smart in appearance. Brim is made to turn down to form a Storm proof hat as shown. Close fitting, light, cloth appearance, neutral colour, absolutely waterproof, and no leakage is possible. 4/11

With small Brim 3/11

All our Garments guaranteed well made and wearing parts specially strengthened

Agents:
Mr. FREDERICK PLUCK.
Complete Outfitter.
BRAINTREE, ESSEX.

Messrs. S. & H. BANBURY,
HIGH ST., DORKING.

THE "YOKE SMOCK" is a well-designed Farm Smock, smart in appearance, and can be worn with the Standard Outfit. In Amazon 11/9, Mercerised Casement 12/11, Plain Zephyr 13/11, Khaki Jean 13/11, Munition Brown Jean 14/11.

THE "AGRICOLA" OUTFIT, as illustrated, is an ideal landworker's outfit, well and smartly made. All wearing parts are specially strengthened and always give satisfaction. Price, in Superior Quality Khaki Jean, Overall (40 in. long) and Breeches (small, medium or large) 18/11. Puttees, per pair, 2/11. Hat (Khaki Jean or Waterproof), 3/11.

THE "STANDARD" Outfit is well designed and made. It is buckled at the waist and fits closely, thus permitting work to be done in ease and comfort. The "Agricola" Overall, the Coat Smock and the Yoke Smock can be worn with this outfit. The Hat, which can be obtained in Khaki Jean or Waterproof Cloth, is smart, comfortable and shady. Coat ("Agricola," Coat Smock or Yoke Smock), 13/11, Breeches 10/11, Puttees 2/6, Shirt 6/11, Hat 3/11.
COMPLETE OUTFIT 35/-

Although War conditions will not permit us to send goods on approval, you obtain equal assurance of value by our guarantee of satisfaction or money returned in full.

ALL GOODS SENT POST FREE.   WRITE AT ONCE FOR ILLUSTRATED LIST

THE CLEVELAND MANUFACTURING COMPANY
54d, CLEVELAND ST., FITZROY SQ., LONDON, W.1
(Proprietors: Chamberlain & Co., Ltd.)

Please mention THE LANDSWOMAN when writing to Advertisers.

An advertisement from *The Landswoman*, November 1918, representative of many which appeared in the magazine.

about eighteen. I stayed there, ploughing. When the news came through on the day the war finished I was digging potatoes in a field. I had a cup of tea to celebrate, then carried on until the boys came home."

The working day of the land army girl comprised nine or ten hours' hard work, normally starting well before dawn, for which she received a shilling wage. Carol Twinch continues:-

"There were mangolds and turnips to be pulled and topped by hand, loaded by fork, and then carted by horse to be clamped in a frost-free 'cave' to serve as winter fodder. Hand milking was a necessity, carried out in the early morning and again at night, after a long day in the fields. There were cold mornings, frozen fingers, and there was little reliable light. Mud-caked skirts took hours to dry in often damp, draughty rooms, while hot water might entail a long wait for a very little."

It is astonishing that so many had been willing to accept the often appalling living and working conditions involved in keeping the nation fed. Not for the Land Army the companionship of the other women's services. Instead they were asked to accept low pay, a pitifully inadequate uniform only grudgingly given and, for some, an unfamiliar isolation within a rural community which seemed to belong to another age.

The *Landswoman* magazine tried to offer incentives for recruitment, both by offering praise and suggesting that the uniform of the land girl was both glamorous and acceptable by giving it the accolade of the President of the Board of Agriculture:-

"There is nothing frivolous in instancing the admirable choice of the woman-like yet becoming uniform of the Land Army. Even Victorian prejudice grows reconciled to the dress or finds solace in the reflection that it is very Greek."

The Women's Land Army was demobilised on 30th November, 1919. Writing in the *Landswoman*, Lord Lee conveyed his official thanks:-

WOMEN'S LAND ARMY.

CONDITIONS AND TERMS.

There are three Sections of the Women's Land Army:

(1). AGRICULTURE.
(2). TIMBER CUTTING.
(3). FORAGE.

If you sign on for A YEAR and are prepared to go wherever you are sent, you can join which Section you like.

YOU PROMISE—

1. To sign on in the Land Army for ONE YEAR.
2. To come to a Selection Board when summoned.
3. To be medically examined, free of cost.
4. To be prepared if PASSED by the Selection Board to take up work after due notice.
5. TO BE WILLING TO GO TO WHATEVER PART OF THE COUNTRY YOU ARE SENT.

THE GOVERNMENT PROMISES—

1. AN INITIAL WAGE to workers of 20/- a week. After they have passed an efficiency test the wages given are 22/- a week and upwards.
2. A short course of FREE INSTRUCTION if necessary.
3. FREE UNIFORM.
4. FREE MAINTENANCE in a Depot for a term not exceeding 4 weeks if the worker is OUT OF EMPLOYMENT through no fault of her own.
5. FREE RAILWAY travelling, when taking up or changing Employment.

——————— OR. ———————

If you sign on for only six months, you can join the Agricultural and Timber Cutting Sections, but not the Forage.

YOU PROMISE—

1. To sign on in the Land Army for 6 MONTHS.
2. To come to a Selection Board when summoned.
3. To be medically examined, free of cost.
4. To be prepared if PASSED by the Selection Board to take up work after due notice.
5. TO BE WILLING TO GO TO ANY PART OF THE COUNTRY YOU ARE SENT.

THE GOVERNMENT PROMISES—

1. AN INITIAL WAGE of 20/- per week.
2. UNIFORM FREE.
3. FREE MAINTENANCE in a Depot for a term not exceeding 2 weeks, if the worker is out of employment through no fault of her own.
4. FREE RAILWAY travelling when taking up or changing employment.

NOTE.—No training is given, therefore the initial wage is only 20/-. Should the worker be able to pass an efficiency test it will be raised to 22/-. Two weeks' maintenance in a depot only is allowed.

Conditions and terms set out for those volunteering to serve in the 1917 Women's Land Army.

146

"Without the aid of women the manhood of the nation could not have withstood the attacks of our enemies, and the Women's Land Army is entitled to a specially honourable place among the various bodies into which women were organised."

Hall Caine's munitions book - *Our Girls* - which is a highly propagandist, government-sponsored idealisation of women's work in the munitions factories, was published in 1917. It does, however, give a detailed picture of the working lives of the 'munitionettes', even if written in a rosy glow of patriotism, and from a totally male point of view:-

"Every instinct of our nature revolts against the thought that woman, with the infinitely delicate organisation which provides for her maternal functions, should under any circumstances whatever take part in the operations such scenes require."

"But Woolwich has a world of operations that are entirely suitable to women, and in a few minutes' more we are in the midst of them. Two thousand women are here, and there is room for three thousand in all. Innumerable lathes, generally of small size, cover the cemented floor, with pulleys and wheels spinning in the air above them. Although most of the machines in this shop are small, some are large and a few are alarming. Here is a slip of a girl working one of the latter kind, a huge thing that has two large wheels like mill-wheels revolving at either side of her, and though she looks like a child in the jaws of some great black monster, she does not seem to be the least afraid."

"One woman is turning base plates for shells on a turret lathe. Another is cutting copper bands for shells from tubes. Another is pressing the copper bands into their places. Yet another is riveting brass plugs on to high explosive shell bodies..."

"All the women wear the same uniform, a khaki-coloured overall girdled at the waist and a cap of the shape

Girl operating vertical milling machine on machine tool parts.

Women packing T.N.T.

of a bathing-cap. This is in the interests of safety, lest the dress or the hair of the operator should be caught in the pulleys and belts of the machinery... Their hard work does not seem to be doing much harm to their health, for their eyes are bright, their cheeks are fresh, and there is hardly any evidence of fatigue among them. They work day and night, in two shifts of twelve hours each, with a break for an hour for dinner and half an hour for tea. Their pay, which is by the piece, is generally large, the minimum being, I think, a pound a week, and the maximum five to seven pounds... It is approaching midnight, but so far as we can see there is no weariness anywhere. The girls look fresh and bright, in their overalls and caps, and when the steam-whistle is sounded at twelve for their midnight dinner, they fly off to their canteen amid a chatter of tongues like children let loose from school."

This romanticised picture, drawn for the purposes of recruitment, contrasts noticeably with the actual lives of the munitions workers. For example, the concentration of labour in the munitions centres brought a heavy pressure on available accommodation. It was not unusual for the same bed to be in use day and night first for a night-shift worker, then for a day-shift worker. In many cases, the worker, man or woman, might have long distances to travel each day, which, when added to the overtime hours frequently worked, might leave barely six hours available for sleep. As previously mentioned, Margaret, who worked at Woolwich Arsenal, said that they were often so tired at night they used to lie on the ammunition. Arthur Marwick, in *Women at War*, gives details of the dangerous and physically damaging effects of working in the munitions factories, taken from an account by two women medical officers, writing in the *Lancet*, 12th August 1916:-

"Throat and/or chest tight, sore, swollen and burning; coughing, sometimes a thick yellow phlegm with bitter taste; pain around waist and in abdomen; nausea, vomiting, constipation at first, then diarrhoea; rashes and eruptions on skin. These could in turn lead to toxic symptoms: digestive, as in the irritative stage in jaundice; circulatory, giddiness, hot and cold flushes, swelling etc.; cerebral drowsiness, loss of memory, disorders of sight; delirium, coma and convulsions."

There was later some attention directed to problems of fatigue, sickness and nutrition. In the case of girls living, or daily travelling, far from home, there was felt to be an especially strong case for the establishment of welfare supervisors. Women working on TNT ran grave health risks and were nicknamed 'canaries' as they developed a yellow discoloration of the skin. For them a free daily pint of milk was provided.

Seventy-one women munitions workers were killed in explosions, sixty-one died of poisoning, and other accidents killed eighty-one women.

The above are three examples of the type of work that women in wartime took on with remarkable efficiency and ease of adjustment. There is no mention whatsoever of any of these jobs in the magazines. The world of work and the world of the magazines remained realms apart...

Those who had returned to domesticity remained as much indoors as they had been before the war, and the sense of independence they had experienced during the war vanished as swiftly as it had come. Women were particularly encouraged to forget any new ideas they had entertained about their place in the world. Women's magazines focused on creating their own idea of a successful woman. Quintessentially feminine, she busied herself around the house far more than her mother had done. She dabbled in a little creative cooking, dainty sewing, intelligent mothering and, above all, she ran a beautiful home.

CHAPTER VIII

The War in the Magazines – The War in Reality:

"The trench is like a slaughterhouse – I am the only woman out of forty to escape."

Continuing on the theme of propaganda, the placing of the wounded hero between the magazine pages represented a need to prove the topicality of war – although detailed descriptions of actual wounds or physical suffering could not be allowed to upset the reader. The propaganda element remained a 'home-centred' one. The magazines often used the war as a means of effecting unrealistic reconciliations between husbands and wives, softening their natures and leading to romantic conclusions. War was topical, and was therefore brought into the stories in the magazines, as in *The Englishwoman*, November 1916, but no mention was made of actual events:-

"The advent of Johnny and Bill was indeed a great event in the village. They were considered a trifle disappointing in that they could rarely be induced to talk of the rigours they had endured."

Neither was there any mention of the immense human suffering, the heartbreaking anxieties, and the grief-stricken homes, nor the fate of millions of soldiers maimed with shrapnel and bullets; or the legacy of 'shell shock' among even those not physically wounded.

The war was also often used as the means of bringing a peaceful conclusion to the story, as in *Home Chat*, July 1915:-

"He was tired, so tired, and his head hung limply; but his eyes looked straight ahead, as if seeking a haven of rest. He walked with the aid of a stick, for one leg was straight and stiff... He was almost dead with the long walk, and so weak that I had to lead him to an armchair – his armchair... 'I've come home', he said."

Tit Bits was not averse to giving what was probably considered the 'human touch' within its pages:-

> "In the village of Bilton, near Rugby, are three mothers, living within a hundred yards of one another, each of whom has lost a son in the war. In two cases the youngest son has been taken; in the third, the youngest but one."

A great deal of different kinds of literary discourse written both during and, for a decade at least, after the war, shows itself to be strongly in opposition to the propaganda element in the magazines. This was particularly obvious in its determination to bring to the fore through the writers' own perceptions and experiences the actual events that took place at the battlefront, and the immensity of the social and psychological changes that so rapidly occurred. There is now a huge area of writing to examine in this context, with some widely known examples of poetry, novels and autobiographical work by male writers, not only those who took part in the war, but of the generation that immediately followed; they were also emotionally affected by it.

Women writers, too, used their work to examine the psychological effects of the horrors of war upon the lives of returning soldiers and their families. Rebecca West in *Return of the Soldier* and Virginia Woolf in *Mrs Dalloway* offer heartbreaking examples of the psychological devastation of the war:-

Chris comes back from the war suffering from amnesia, brought on by shell shock. He has blocked out the fifteen years of his life that have followed the love affair which brought him real happiness, and has tried to return to that previous stage in his life. When he is considered to be 'cured' he returns to the front:-

> "Chris walked across the lawn. He was looking up under his brows at the over-arching house as though it were a hated place to which, against all his hopes, business had forced him to return. He stepped aside to avoid a patch of brightness cast by a lighted window on the grass; lights in our house were worse than darkness, affection worse than hate elsewhere. He wore a dreadful decent smile; I knew how his voice would resolutely lift in greeting us. He

walked not loose-limbed like a boy... but with the soldier's hard tread upon the heel... When we had lifted the yoke of our embraces from his shoulders he would go back to that flooded trench in Flanders under that sky more full of flying death than clouds, to that No Man's Land where bullets fall like rain on the rotting faces of the dead." *Return of the Soldier*

Septimus Smith has also returned from the war:-

"When the damned fool came again, Septimus refused to see him. 'Did he indeed?' said Dr Holmes. 'So you are in a funk,' he said agreeably, sitting down at his patient's side. He had actually talked of killing himself to his wife, quite a girl, a foreigner, wasn't she?... For he had forty years' experience behind him; and Septimus could take Dr Holmes's word for it – there was nothing whatever the matter with him.
So he was deserted. The whole world was clamouring: 'Kill yourself, kill yourself, for our sakes!' But why should he kill himself for their sakes? Besides, now that he was quite alone, condemned, deserted, as those who are about to die are alone, there was a luxury in it, an isolation full of sublimity; a freedom which the attached can never know... (He) flung himself vigorously, violently down on to Mrs Filmer's area railings." *Mrs Dalloway*

It is, of course, difficult to judge how the literature which, for the most part, appeared *after* the war would have emotionally affected readers had it been placed before them at a time when their own relatives were being killed or wounded. In addition, one cannot judge whether the political and strategic confusion which occurred could have been so successfully hidden from the general public, if the facts of the news from the battle front had been allowed to be placed before them at the time they had actually occurred.

The depiction of women in the magazines, in terms of a publishing and editorial picture of how 'she' appears – or how 'she' should behave – is offered a more startling contrast by using the work of

155

women writers, and their experiences of the war as it affected them, and as they saw it.

As has been discussed, the romantic stories in the magazines abstracted the heroic, even elegiac, attributes of war, and the articles, both editorial and contributory, concentrated on home front involvement in helping the war effort, or wrote 'human interest' features which, to a modern reading, appear extraordinarily naïve in both their approach and their apparent belief that their readers would readily accept them:-

> "His love for children makes Tommy the idol of rural France, which admires him as a fighter and a man, with that unquenchable spirit which has been such a really valuable asset to the Allied armies... He has fed refugees, young and old, for days out of his own plentiful rations; tiny girls were seen toddling at his side wearing the 'woollies' and comforters which loving fingers had made for him in that village of his own in England. Our soldiers have drawn their pay, of course, whilst on campaign, but so well fed have they been, and so completely supplied with comforts... that the French children have come in for many a treat... all the orders that ever were issued would not keep a Thomas Atkins from making friends with the children." *Home Chat* January 1919

Vera Brittain was among the radical social critics whose work drew on the immense social changes that took place. She describes the scene in Buxton on the outbreak of war – a microcosm of what was happening all over England at the time:-

> "The German cousins of some local acquaintances left the town in a panic. My parents... laid in stores of cheese, bacon and butter under the generally shared impression that by next week we might all be besieged by the Germans. Wild rumours circulated from mouth to mouth... One or two Buxton girls were hurriedly married to officers summoned to unknown destinations. Pandemonium swept over the town. Holiday trippers wrestled with one another for the Daily Mail; habitually quiet and respectable citizens

TOMMY'S FRIENDS. *[Official.*

Tommy Atkins' love for children has made
him the idol of rural France. He may not
understand the language, but he makes
friends with the children all the same.
These little French girls only escaped death
by a few yards, the house next to theirs
being smashed to atoms.

struggled like wolves for the provisions in the food shops, and vented upon the distracted assistants their dismay at hearing that all prices had suddenly gone up."

The Year 1914 Illustrated however, plays down this state of panic out of a sense of patriotism:-

"Our food supply: in the early days of the war there were signs of a threatened panic among a section of the community consequent on the expectation of a shortage of our food supply. This panic showed itself in private individuals laying in large stores of food, and the consequent raising of prices by the traders. This course was at once denounced as unpatriotic, and persons indulging in greed at the expense of their neighbours were threatened with dire consequences. To protect the consumer, the Government issued a standard sale price for certain articles and also bought up the whole of the sugar stocks. This action had the desired effect, and very little inconvenience was caused to the majority of householders by reason of the shortage of supplies."

Vera Brittain in *Testament of Youth*, as above, writes later in the war on the results of the upheavals at home:-

"I wrote to my family on January 10th, 1917... 'from everyone's people come exactly the same sort of letters as I get from you. Everyone is servantless, no one visits anyone else or goes away, and the food seems as hard to get hold of in other places as in London now.'"

She tried hard to persuade her parents to keep up their morale, as those serving at the Front were trying so hard to do:-

"But do if you can try to carry on without being too despondent and make other people do the same... for the great fear in the Army and all its appurtenances out here is not that it will ever give up itself, but that the civil population at home will fail us by losing heart – and so of course morale – just at the most critical time. The most critical time is of course now, before America can really come in and the hardships of the winter are not yet over."

The internal state of corruption and injustice in Britain was examined by D.H. Lawrence, particularly in *Kangaroo*. In this novel he tried to point out that the need for conscription showed that there was some degree of opposition to war. The treatment of pacifists was often harsh and unjust, but the recognition of the category at all was a sign of how far moral and religious objections to war were rooted in the English liberal tradition:-

"Many men, carried on a wave of patriotism and true belief in democracy, entered the war. Many men were driven in out of belief that it was necessary to save their property. Vast numbers of men were just bullied into the army. A few remained. Of these, many became conscientious objectors... Most came back home victorious in circumstance, but with their inner pride gone... To come back home, many of them, to wives who had egged them on to this downfall in themselves. Others to return to a bewildered wife who had in vain tried to keep her man true to himself, tried and tried, only to see him at last swept away."

Few novelists of the post-war period attempted to bypass the major events of contemporary history. For the generation that was just too young to fight, whose memories of 1914-1918 were complicated by the emotions of boredom and guilt, the war provided special images of horror, attitudes to war and its presentation in literature. Noel Coward, Somerset Maugham and Evelyn Waugh were among these.

Vera Brittain referred to the failure of reputable authors to give adequate acknowledgement of the extent of women's involvement in the war effort. Authors like Edmund Blunden, Siegfried Sassoon, Robert Graves and David Jones recorded their personal experiences of combat; apart from references to prostitutes, café proprietresses, and loved ones at home, women seemed hardly to come into the picture – as shown below.

Richard Aidington's *Death of a Hero* portrayed his female characters as grotesque or superficial:-

"Although a lady of 'mature charms', Mrs Winterbourne loved to fancy herself as a delicious young thing of seventeen... She was a mistress of would-be revolutionary platitudes about marriage and property... but in fact, was as sordid, avaricious, conventional and spiteful a middle-class woman as you could dread to meet.

Like all her class, she toadied to her betters and bullied her inferiors.

The meeting with Fanny was somehow a failure. She was extremely gay and pretty and well-dressed and charming, and talked cheerily at first, and then valiantly against his awkward silences. He seemed to have nothing to say to Fanny... he missed half her witty sayings and clever allusions... Yet he was very fond of Fanny, very fond of her, just as he was very fond of Elizabeth. And yet he seemed to have so little to say to them, and found it so hard to follow their careless intellectual chatter. He had tried to tell Elizabeth some of his War experiences. Just as he was describing the gas bombardment and the awful look on the faces of the men gassed, he noticed her delicate mouth was wried by a suppressed yawn."

The bitterness felt by soldiers against the non-combatants, which he depicted, was understandable, though it was unfair to blame women in general for the social conventions that kept them out of the trenches. Many women, particularly ambulance drivers, nurses and VADs, were very close to trench warfare, and were killed by bombs or wounded by shelling. For example, at Abbéville on 29th and 30th May 1918, nine WAAC workers were killed by bombs, and next day several nurses were killed at Étaples. Helen Zenna Smith – a pseudonym for Evadne Price, a journalist, playwright and children's author – in *Not So Quiet* apparently drew on a diary of the work of an ambulance driver at the French Front. This was a bitterly ironic 'piece of opportunism' produced in England as an answer to Erich Maria Remarque's book *All Quiet on the Western Front*, which had

Shell Bursting on Hospital
at Lierre.

achieved such enormous world-wide success when published in 1929 that a flood of war books ensued.

As a 'first person account' *Not So Quiet* is a searing indictment of the brutality of war. It denounces 'armchair patriotism', showing that for those who witnessed the consequences of battle, war service was a 'passkey to scenes of devastation and atrocity which civilian glory-seekers could never visualise':-

> "How we dread the morning clean-out of the inside of our cars [ambulances], we gently-bred, educated women they insist on so rigidly for this work that apparently cannot be done by women incapable of speaking English with a public-school accent!
>
> ...The stench that comes out as we open the doors each morning nearly knocks us down... blood and mud and vermin and the stale stench of stinking trench feet and gangrenous wounds. Pour souls, they cannot help it. No one blames them.
>
> The trench is like a slaughterhouse. All round me girls are lying dead or dying. Some are wounded. The wounded are trying to staunch one another's blood. A few are shell-shocked. The roll is called. The casualties are heavy. Ten dead, two missing, twenty-four injured... I am the only woman out of forty to escape."

Yet the letters she receives from home and family are echoes of the stories in the women's magazines:-

> "Darling, what an inestimable privilege you have, marrying one of England's disabled heroes, devoting your life to his service! No orange blossoms or anything like that – I think it would be bad form – but a smart grey frock and hat...
>
> I am grief-stricken, but I feel I must write to tell you of Roy's splendid achievement – how he got his MC... As soon as he is strong enough he goes to Buckingham Palace for the investiture – a great honour – and the King will personally thank him for his bravery... He is, of course, a

trifle depressed, but that will wear off once he is out of hospital and has been decorated... I am proud of his blindness and disability... and I thank God for blessing me among all women for mothering a hero."

The letter from her fiancé confirms the reality of the situation:-

"Dear Nell,
    The nurse is writing this for obvious reasons. Mother will have told you about my eyes and my leg, but there is something she hasn't told you because she doesn't know. There will never be any perambulator on that lawn of ours, Nell... You're brick enough to stand the blindness and the limp, but the other is too much to ask any woman. So I release you from your promise... I haven't cared about anything for a long time. I only wish to Christ they'd left me another five minutes in the trench."

This black satire had three British editions in two years, was published in French translation by the firm of Gallimard, was turned into a play and staged, and had a sequel in 1931 entitled *Women of the Aftermath*.

Vera Brittain, in *Testament of Youth*, Irene Rathbone in *We That Were Young*, and Radclyffe Hall in *The Well of Loneliness* are three other women authors who were determined to describe the conditions under which women worked during the war at the Front, in contrast to the magazines' secure, well-ordered picture of women's lives at home, which the suffering and disorder of the fighting and dying did not seem to touch. Somewhere in the enormous gap between the stories in the magazines and the novels of the above authors lie the testimonies of those who were at home in England, and remember with unnerving detail what took place seventy-five years ago. Jane was one of them:-

"I was married in 1917. My husband had seven days' leave. When I saw him off at Victoria Station I was so upset by a train of wounded soldiers that came in, I could not go back to work. I got the sack."

Margaret was another:-

"I had been married a fortnight when my husband fell in the door, having been ill all the time. He had malaria, dysentery, had been gassed and shot through the back. When I visited him in hospital he showed me the wound – it had *paper* on it. I said, 'Come home, don't stop here.' He just walked out of the hospital. I went back. Sister 'carried on': 'What are you going to live on?' Our savings had all gone."

"I saw the Lady Almoner, told her I was tearing up sheets for the wound. 'Come on Fridays, I will give you 7/6d and dressings.' I went to work every morning for Lady C. I was so tired, had no sleep, could smell the wound all the time. Her daughter told me to get some incense from the chemist. I had no drugs for him – I went to the pub every day to get a drop of brandy for him to ease the pain. Lady C paid for a taxi for him to go back to hospital. In three months he had wasted away."

Dorothy Moriarty, in her memoirs, also looked back seventy-five years to memories of absolute clarity:-

"Like most dreamers faced with grim reality, I was weary and disillusioned as I closed the doors of Ward 8 behind me and joined the stream of nurses on their way to second supper. But I also felt that life had taken on a new meaning. Before I undressed that night I set the photograph of my three brothers – taken in those first frantic weeks of war – on top of my chest of drawers. I looked proudly at the three khaki-clad figures, all doing their bit in conditions far worse than I would ever know. I would give them no cause to be ashamed of me, I was in the war effort now, and I would stick it out.

"Looking back, I realise what a very small world was that of a probationer nurse. Outside the red-brick walls of our hospital, across the English Channel a war was raging. And yet, except when one of our menfolk came home on leave, or a Zeppelin raid robbed us of sleep, or there was

the name of someone we knew in the casualty lists, we were
smothered in trivia that obscured the larger issues – the war,
with all its far-reaching consequences…"

CHAPTER IX

Biographies

While many fragments of information gleaned from the women interviewed have already been interwoven into the previous chapters, this method has not made it possible to give more biographical pictures of their lives. They have all survived to a very great age, and a certain amount of initial diffidence soon dissolved as they were encouraged to talk about themselves with very little prompting or interruption. Placed into context, their stories are both fascinating and, in many cases, uplifting, as with courage and humour they constantly surprised and delighted. I am very grateful for having had the opportunity to meet and talk with them.

MARY:
Mary was born in 1897. She was seen at a home for the elderly in York.

"I started working at the Rowntree's factory in 1916, when I was fourteen years old, working in the packing room, packing blocks of plain chocolate for the troops, I can see the trays now – putting the seals on the top and bottom of the boxes. We lived in a small village. There were four children in the family. We were not really desperate for food. Mother baked bread – there was always a bowl of dough on the steel fender. I baked bread when I was twelve."

"We did not go out. Mother scrubbed and washed all day. I helped her when I was not working. I was not one to gad about. My younger sister learned to play the piano – it was my job to keep it clean! 'Have you done the table legs?' my mother asked. 'Lift one leg up at a time and stand it in your bucket!' I remember *My Weekly*. I liked waiting for the next week, waiting for the serials and the funny bits, and the problem pages – it was only a few coppers. We passed them on, one to another."

"I did not do anything for the war effort. It was quiet during the war, with no bombing. My father was a rough-riding sergeant, in a riding school, training horses and men for the cavalry. He brought horses into the 'Remount Depot'. I remember him going to the Front. He brought back three brass bomb cases, as souvenirs, which had fancy engraving on them, done by the Chinese Labour Corps(?) in Belgium. They were solid brass. The end of the biggest one had been shaped like a serviceman's cap, with a crown on the top."

"After the war, I stayed on at Rowntree's until I got married. Everything changed after the war."

JOAN:

Joan was born in 1898. She was seen at the same time as Mary.

"We lived in a village. There were eight of us in the family at the beginning of the war. Each village had its own searchlight. The German Zeppelins used to come over. We lived beside a church with a very high steeple so we used to go and sleep in a cottage by the river, in case the church was bombed."

"We were a farming family, so we had no food shortages. One of my brothers worked on the land, and did not have to go to war. The other women in the village were very bitter about this, so my brother used to go out the back door to the fields, so as not to be seen."

"Life did not change for us during the war. I did nothing for the war effort. I was too busy to read magazines."

"Three of my brothers were in the war. One was wounded, but did not want to talk about it."

DOROTHY:

Dorothy was born in 1903. She was also seen in York.

"I was eleven when the war started. The women in the village worked in their homes, then on the land, so we could not get domestic help any more. The government altered the clocks, putting them two hours on, to give more daylight."

"At eleven years of age, at school, we had to write to the Kaiser as a composition. I wrote it by myself. The head teacher said it was so good, it was printed in the local paper, the *Selby Times*. My mother was very proud of me:-

'It is beneath me to write to you at all, but as I have to do it, I will make the best of it.

How is your son the Crown Prince? We call him the Clown Prince. I hope (?) will change their minds and go with the Old Firm.

Yours in disgust, an English schoolgirl.'"

"I've never thought about that for seventy-five years!"

"My brother always put me in my place. He told me, 'When the Germans get here, you will be the first to be killed!'"

"I left school at thirteen. I remember a plane crashing nearby. I remember running 1½ miles to see it. The three soldiers inside were billeted on us for three weeks. One was an officer's batman, in his thirties. I had to give up my room. It was very difficult to feed them – my mother had recently died. I had to make them breakfast and heard them say to each other, 'Don't we get rotten food here?' and to me, 'Don't tell your sister what we said.' We had nothing to give them. The people in the cities were in very bad shape."

"I had to cook – one of my brothers, who was married, came for dinner. We had a wood-burning stove. I made a rabbit pie while the stove was hot; then some Eccles cakes, but it had cooled down. My brother said, 'What are these anaemic things?'"

"There was a lot of propaganda in wartime on *both* sides. We had *Pearson's Weekly*, and did the competitions. I liked *Tit Bits* and occasionally *Vogue*. I imagined myself dressed in the clothes – I had ½d a week to spend."

"There was a regiment of soldiers staying in York. I was 'in love' with one of them. When they were leaving I said, 'I am going out to see Captain... and wave goodbye to him.' My friend said, 'He won't look at you,' but he did and he smiled at me...'"

"We had meetings for young men to volunteer. I sang solo with my school in village halls. One particular evening I sang 'Oh, we don't want to lose you, but we think you ought to go.' One young man stood up and said, 'I'll make one.' He enlisted and was killed within one week. I was very upset. I felt responsible. I still do. I put everything into my singing."

"We went round the villages collecting eggs for wounded soldiers. We gave concerts to raise money for wounded soldiers. They called me 'little Miss Lavender'."

"My older brothers went into munitions – they were not fit enough for the army."

ETHEL:

Aged ninety-three, Ethel was seen in a home for the elderly in Hampshire.

men in skilled jobs but promised this would only be for the duration of the war. Managers were delighted. Not only was a woman cheaper but, as a manager of a munitions factory observed, she adapted instantly to the new assembly lines.

On mass production she will come first every time ... we were never able to get the men to cope with it.... Men will not stand the monotony of a fast repetition job like women, they will not stand by a machine pressing buttons all their lives, but a woman will.

Four hundred thousand domestic servants left their jobs for the more popular factory work, including Ethel Dean. Landing a job on munitions at Woolwich Arsenal was the break she had been waiting for. She was thankful not to become one of the 'canary girls' working with TNT which had serious side effects and turned the workers yellow. Her own job was hazardous enough. Surrounded by barrels of gunpowder it took little to set off an explosion so every morning Ethel had to strip off her clothes and wear regulation overalls, a special hat and shoes. 'You wasn't allowed to wear any hairpins in your hair, no hooks and eyes in your clothes, nothing metal whatever on you, even linen buttons with metal rings.' Many of the girls working on shell-filling with Ethel suffered from abdominal pains and nausea.

Despite its drawbacks, Ethel found life in a munitions factory far more fun than domestic service had ever been. The pay was better too although,

"I was born with rickets, we were so short of food. I was bow-legged until I was four or five."

"I worked in service before the war. We had no hot water, no Hoovers, just a long brush for the carpets, etc. We had to carry coal up four or five flights of stairs – a sackful for each fire, and scrub the steel fenders with emery board."

"When the young men servants enlisted I went to Woolwich Arsenal. It was too hard for us to fill up and carry the coal scuttles. Previously I had been on board wages. We had to buy our own food out of 12s 6d per week. We had to have three uniform dresses, six yards each, of print material. I had to make them myself. I had no spare time for reading; I could not afford magazines on 3s 4d a week wages. I used to go to Selfridges on my afternoon off. I used to stand at the perfume counter, looking at the bottles of Californian Poppy perfume. I could not afford one – they cost 2s 6d each."

"During the war I lived in different lodgings. One of my landladies only gave me a herring for my supper after work. There was no canteen at the Arsenal – I had to take my own teapot, though we could get hot water."

"I found it strange in the Arsenal because I had to do sewing. I had to weigh the cordite and balastite flakes and put them into bags, which went behind the shells and were forced out. We were paid according to what the munitions shop produced. Patriotism? I had a job and that was it. The girls in the Arsenal did not talk about the war. I lived in lodgings in Plumstead. I had a long journey. I left the factory after 7 p.m. and got home after eight."

"After the war, I would not go back into service so I went to work in a pub. I was not allowed to speak to the customers. My husband (I met him in the pub after the war) was a skilled fitter from Lancashire. He worked on guns in the Woolwich Arsenal."

ELIZABETH:

Elizabeth was seen in a home for the elderly in Hendon.

"I was born in 1892. I am ninety-nine. I lived in Edmonton. My father shod bus and tram horses. We were eight children in the family. I was the youngest. I stayed at home, did not work until I answered an advertisement for a maternity nurse. I had no training."

"I was engaged, but my fiancé was killed in the war. I never married."

171

The party of the century

All smiles ... Elizabeth Fowler celebrates her 100th birthday

693106

ELIZABETH FOWLER of Finchley celebrated her 100th birthday this week surrounded by friends old and new.

A former nanny and maternity nurse, Edmonton-born Elizabeth lived and worked in Finchley before retiring 40 years ago. But she is still visited loyally at Beach Lodge, Hendon Lane, Finchley, by some of the young children she helped bring up — now middle-aged.

And while she remembers the good times, such as visits to the Gaumont Cinema, she also remembers how hard the work was: "It was very tiring, and it was very poor pay at times."

Picture by PETER BEAL

At Beach Lodge Elizabeth keeps everyone entertained with songs. But her sweet, happy singing hides a weight of sadness: her fiance was killed in action during the First World War, and she says she never found a man to compare to him.

The watch he gave her before he went off to fight more than 75 years ago is still one of her most treasured possessions, and she carries it with her wherever she goes, in memory of the man she had taken from her by war.

"I remember some of the magazines. I made my own clothes, and was very fond of cooking – my mother taught me."

SYBIL:

Sybil was nearly ninety-two when seen. She has been on the television programme *Out of the Dolls House*. She was interviewed at Victoria Bus Station, on her way to a meeting of the Guide Movement.

"As one of the longest serving members of the [Girl Guide] Movement, and being a founder member, which takes me back to 1910, and being ninety-one years old, almost ninety-two, perhaps I am in a position to remember the magazines."

"The *Guide Gazette* was my first love and the *Boys Own* came a good second. I was at school when war broke out, at Clapham High School – one year and then went to Dartmouth in Kent to our best Training College in PE. I was married before the end of the war but had to see my husband return to France and I returned to my teaching job. PE, Anatomy, Hygiene, etc., etc.. It was wonderful to be doing the work I really cared about and teach students how to teach their pupils to enjoy PT and the games associated with it. This has helped me all my life and I can still take a Brownie Pack or Guide Company in rousing games that they all enjoy."

"You will be interested to know that I am off to a big Guide meeting in Melbourne, Australia and then to Tasmania to meet my grandchildren and great grandchildren in September. Propose to come back via California. Not bad for nearly ninety-two!"

"I married in 1918. I was a student and teacher at seventeen during the war. I read magazines, but not the serials. My mother made my clothes. I scrubbed floors in King's College Hospital during the war. While still at school I took a barrow and collected old iron for recycling. I collected stamps, envelopes and note paper to write letters for soldiers in hospital or to give them to write themselves."

"Patriotism was encouraged through the Church and clubs, to push volunteers to enlist or feel guilty. Class differences – not noticed in magazines, but as teachers we expected it. Sexual attitudes shown in magazines, very traditional and rigid – I am still. I read the problem pages in magazines. There was no problem taking over jobs. Some did not step back when the men returned. I did not notice propaganda posters. The magazines did bring the war home, but a lot was

173

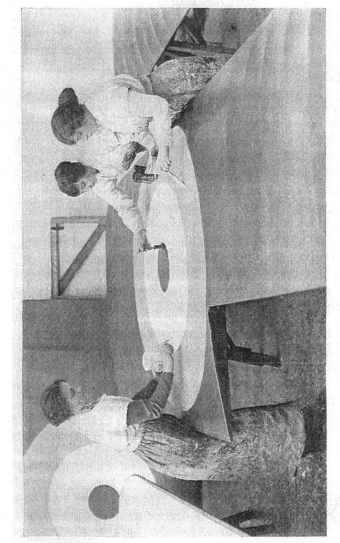

Painting identification rings on aeroplanes.

suppressed as well. I was not affected by what I read in the magazines, I have good memories of the magazines. It was an escape as things were difficult. The information was useful on fashion, health, recreation, ideas for the home. The fiction was a fantasy world. They dealt with the consequences of war – e.g.: how to make eggless cakes. The stories always ended happily."

JANE:

Jane was seen at a home for the elderly in Greenford.

"I was born on 14th November, 1893. I was fourteen when I went to work. I had won a scholarship, but my mother could not afford the uniform. We were a large family, eight brothers and sisters. I did not have time to read, and my mother did not encourage us to do so. I liked school – didn't have disagreements like the kids have now! All my brothers fought in the war. The eldest was an officer. One was blinded in one eye."

"When the 1914 war broke out I was twenty-one on 14th November. I was working at J. Lyons tea shop at 215 Oxford Street, London."

"We were directed to war work. I went to the Aircraft Manufacturing Co. at Colindale, Hendon, and was put to work in the upholstery department at first stuffing large cushions with horsehair for Swifts flying boat. That was the funny thing – they were going out to be bombed anyway. We worked long hours and overtime, I had to take a workman's ticket to Colindale – 3d. The horsehair was sterilised but not too good to look at. After this we did doors and cushions for De Havilland Aircraft."

"I remember Miss Margaret Bonfield coming to Hendon with her banners, 'Women of the World Unite', to form the first union for better wages, which were then 13s a week (old money) and extra for overtime."

"I remember King George and Queen Mary with Princess Mary coming to visit the factory in 1915. Queen Mary came in shabby clothes so that she did not upset anyone, and to set an example. Mr G De Havilland and his co-designer used a mock-up of a plane's engine in front of our bench to test a missile firing through the centre of the propeller."

"We had an air raid warning during the day but nothing happened. But that night an aerial torpedo fell on the railway line between

175

Cricklewood Lane and Mill Lane, West Hampstead, missing the factory at Cricklewood but breaking all the windows on both sides of the railway line. This factory was another aircraft factory. I was shaken over by the explosion on the railway line, as I was on the iron bridge across the line, but not hurt. I got up and ran the rest of the way home to find my sister had put a table in front of the fireplace with bedding on top, but had forgotten about the chimney, and they were covered in soot! I was married on 30th October 1917, and I was discharged for not returning to work on the day my husband returned to France. My husband had had seven days' leave. I saw him off at Victoria, and was so upset by a train of wounded soldiers that came in, I could not go straight back to work that day."

"I then went to work at Schweppes factory, where we sent out thousands of nuts and screws to factories for aircraft. I sent parcels to my husband at the Front – clean underwear scented with lavender – he got the bird! My husband was brought home on a stretcher from France, and sent up North to hospital. When he recovered he went to High Wycombe to a remount depot and was there when the war finished. I went there in 1918 and worked in a furniture factory making trench rattles for gas attacks. They were exactly like football rattles, dipped in creosote."

"On Armistice Day in High Wycombe a chamber pot tied with ribbon was tied to the top of The Red Lion pub sign, and a policeman was tied to the post in the square. We all went mad!"

"I did not really notice women giving up their jobs. Majority got married after the war. The factory girls got married in a church next to the tram sheds depot in Colindale, which was dedicated to soldiers and factory girls. Wartime brought more friendly neighbours, everyone got on well – went back into their shells afterwards."

"I saw one man given a white feather – unfair as people did not really know what others' circumstances were."

GRACE:

Grace was ninety-eight when seen at the same home as Elizabeth, in Hendon.

"*My Weekly* was very popular, particularly the competitions. I read *Girl's Friend*. I was married in 1913, and had two children by 1915, so I could not work. There were shortages of everything. I knitted mittens, knee caps, balaclavas, gloves for soldiers. I sent parcels to the front. I had a brother in the Civil Service who went into the catering corps during the war. He begged for a marrow bone to make soup. I sent one in a parcel; also faggots – the parcel fell to bits when it was opened! I wrote letters, filled with anything you thought of to fill them up. I remember Zeppelins flying low, picked out with searchlights, like some beast in the sky."

"*My Weekly* – I liked the serials and recipes and fashions, and how to bring up children, and how to make jam. They made good housewives of us. Everything was made by hand, nothing wasted. I read magazines to forget what was happening. We were all great readers in our family."

"My husband was a chemist, made special TNT. If they had told us the reason why we should do war work, we could have given information to the enemy. So they did not say much, trying to pretend not much was happening. We were not prepared for the First World War, therefore lots of problems. I remember getting up at five in the morning to queue up for a loaf, and then it was mouldy. I remember that the hansom cabs were called in for the Front."

"Every one of the problem pages in the magazines, either you or your sister or your friend had something like it. We were always looking to see if they'd sorted it out. They never did sort it out. The answers were evasive. Mourning for a year, some families more than others, if you could afford it. Many gone during the war. Black bands worn instead, saved your face that way. I remember the war posters, particularly the Kitchener one – I can picture his face now."

ROSE, MOLLY, SUSAN (interviewed together):

Rose, Molly and Susan were in their late eighties when seen at a home for retired teachers in Elstree.

Molly – "I can remember the pictures in the magazines." Molly knitted balaclavas and scarves which went to soldiers they adopted. Rose worked in Casualty Office. They adopted soldiers, sent parcels (hard boiled eggs, chocolate and tobacco). Groups of girls went to see wounded soldiers in local hospitals although Rose did not go. Did not talk about it. Middle class women helped in hospitals. Molly noticed shortages in the shops.

Rose looked at children's pages in *Home Chat* and the fashions; she was still very young during the war. Molly's mother had *People's Friend*. Rose remembered *Peg's Paper*, also read *Answers* (Horatio

I WAS 5 st. 4 lb. TOO FAT.

Without Exercising, Starving, Sweating, or Dangerous Drugs, I Banished all my Excess Fat In a Very Short Time by a Simple Nature-Cure.

YOU CAN CURE YOUR OBESITY AS EASILY AS I DID.

To Prove What the Remedy Which Cured Me Can Do for Others, I Want Every Reader Who is Too Fat, or Gaining Fat, to Accept To-day a 1s. 6d. Size Box from Me Without Charge or Obligation.

I was 74 lbs. too heavy—a victim of general obesity. I had a fat-loaded face, a heavy double chin, with an immense amount of fat round my neck and rolls of it down my back. My waist and hips were much affected, my arms bulky, bosom podgy, and figure absolutely lost. Every natural instinct was filled

with loathing though these things were to themselves; they were not the worst feature of my case, for my heart was fat-encased, and if I had not got rid of my fat I should probably not have been alive now. Every day saw me in a more serious condition. I fought my obesity not merely because I hated looking fat and ugly, but because my health—my very life itself—demanded it.

My case trepted all the signs of that treacherous enemy of the obese subject—fatty infiltration of the heart.

Mrs. A. MASON.

Only those who have been menaced with such a disease realise the joy I felt when I eventually discovered a remedy which quickly rid me of any unhealthy adipose tissue and restored to me a well-proportioned figure.

I have now been cured for over two years, and my weight and figure have remained normal all that time without taking any remedy whatever.

Every joy that my remedy brought me can be yours for a mere fraction of the trouble and expense it cost me. Let me send you a free box of my cure now, and prove to you that you need no longer remain fat. Please pin the coupon to the sheet bearing your name and address, and post to me to-day. I will also send you my Illustrated Book, telling all about my cure, together with the evidence of those who have already tried it.

WOMEN WHO SHOULD NOT BE MOTHERS.
By JANE DOE.

The mother who sleeps her infant into a "springless" go-cart and sends it out in the care of irresponsible children.

The mother who doses her offspring with teething powders and soothing syrups.

The mother who takes liberties with her baby's digestion by experimenting with all the patent foods on the market.

The mothers who encourage adenoids and malformation of the teeth by permitting their children in infancy to use a "dummy."

The mother who rears her baby on milk given in an old-fashioned tube feeding bottle, and who is not particular how she cleans it.

The mother who crams little feet into ill-fitting and too heavy shoes.

The mother who likes to "harden" her children and see them go barelegged and bare-kneed even in the depth of winter.

The mother who refers to her children as trials instead of treasures, as ties instead of trusts.

The mother who is a "don'ter" from morning till bedtime.

The mothers who leave their children all day to the indifferent and inexperienced care of nurse-girls.

The mother who lets her child lie in the sun or in a strong light without anything to protect its baby eyes from the glare.

The mother who can go out to the evening cinema and leave her children in bed alone in a locked house.

Bottomley, MP for Hackney) and *Tit Bits*. Liked the romantic stories. Susan's mother took *Home Chat* and she read it. She liked the letters pages, though did not agree with the advice! Looking at the old magazines shown to them: Rose liked the weight reducing advertisement and the one that discussed 'Women who should not be mothers'.

Rose did not believe in equal pay at the time, would not join teachers' union, because she felt it was very anti-men. The men had families to support, and needed more money. Does agree with it now. "A lot of women have just as many calls on their money."

Molly said women could not marry beneath them, and with so many men killed therefore they did not marry. Molly got married very late because of the shortage of men after the war. One of Rose's friends went to work on a farm during the war. She married the farmer's son!

Rose's father was in France during the war. Had only sent postcards, with bits crossed out, as they were censored.

Rose remembers going shopping every other day for her mother, at the Home and Colonial Store. Four pounds of sugar cost 7d, a quarter pound of tea 3d, a half pound of butter 3d. She remembers the 2lb jars of jam, made of stone, straight-sided. Rose was interviewed for *Age to Age*: boyfriends had to go, missed by the girls at home. They were buried far from home. So many families affected. Armistice Day: remembered the open buses, American and English soldiers, shouting and excited. Feeling of relief. Her mother worked in a factory making gas masks.

BETTY:

Betty gave an interview as a result of contact through the producer of *Out of the Dolls House*.

"While growing up I led a completely sheltered existence. Neither at school or at home did I have any contact with 'women's magazines' (except possibly the stories in *Home Chat*). After I came down from Oxford I had no interest in them, nor had my mother, with whom I lived; she died at the age of ninety-seven. I gave all my spare time to the Girl Guide Movement, with which I worked for nearly fifty years. Our periodicals were *The London Illustrated* and *The Queen* and *Picture Post*. I read the *Illustrated London News* for the pictures, *Vogue* for the fashions, *Home Chat* for the stories."

"At twenty-one, I helped in Cheltenham Baby Club, looking after toddlers. I helped to organise guiding and brownie packs in slum areas, then the State took over. I became one of the Infant Welfare Ladies, seeing working class mothers, lots of children, as a volunteer. Then I became a Guider. I was in college during the war. I nearly starved. There was no social life during the war. In my vacations I helped with Red Cross work. I was living in St Ives, always in blackout, because of submarines. I remember using oil lamps, no street lights, used torches and lanterns."

"After my degree, I was not very strong. I worked in an office part-time for War Pensions; assisting soldiers when discharged or invalided out, giving information and interviewing them. My brother was in the Air Force. He joined at eighteen. He was given a white feather before he was eighteen. Next term he left school and enlisted. He would not go into the army, felt he was too young to be in command of men. Learnt to fly, rather than wishing to kill anyone. He survived because he was quarantined with spotted fever, but proved to be a carrier."

MILLIE:
Millie was born in 1897. She was also seen at the home in York.

"I worked at Rowntree's making fancy boxes for chocolates. I had plenty of friends. I never married, looked after my mother. I always worked. We had a coal house shelter. I was frightened to go out at night. I would not like it to come again."

DORIS:
Born 1898, and also seen in York.

"I was clever as a little girl, passed a scholarship and was going to be a school teacher but we had no money. Mother reared us with no help. She took in washing, a thing she had never done before. You were either rich or poor in those days, nothing in between. I was always a reader, trying to learn."

"I liked the love stories. I remember *My Weekly*, *Home Chat*, *Red Letter*, and *Tit Bits*. I read comics at 1d each. I liked the fashions and cooking. I was a good sewer, copied the fashions for my doll. My mother bought a hand sewing machine. There was not the money, you had to make the best of it. We used flour bags during the war to make clothes, dyed them different colours for curtains, etc. I read the agony columns, to have a good laugh. Writing about men knocking them about and giving them babies every year. I'd have knocked *him* about. Silly things they asked."

"I worked on a farm during the war. Learnt a lot of things. I did not know a cow from a bull! I learnt to calve a cow, ring pigs and ride a horse. I was then about eighteen. I stayed there, ploughing. The day war finished, when the news came through, I was digging potatoes in a field. Had a cup of tea to celebrate, then carried on until the boys came home."

"I had boyfriends, some of them joined up in the army – quite a lot never came back. I had several cousins and uncles in the navy. Some of my cousins did not come back, though one of those in the navy was torpedoed and did come back. They had problems finding jobs at the end of the war."

"Then I went into service in the big houses. There were six or seven maids in one family. It was hard, with no electrical help. Nothing else for a girl to do. The wages were very poor – 2s per week to start with. I was given material for two print dresses each Christmas in service. I had to supply my own caps and aprons out of my own money."

"I started at 7 a.m. with breakfast for the master, to eight at night scrubbing, cleaning, polishing. I had every other Sunday off after washing the dinner dishes and getting tea ready. I went to see my mother when I had a day off. Every other Sunday we had to go to church. No night off for fear you had a baby. I had no idea what babies were! I did all right – went from one house to another to earn more money."

"I was not bothered about the vote; I had no time. I was the DIY man when I married. I was quite happy with a saw in my hand."

VICTORIA:

Victoria was ninety-nine when interviewed at her house in Hove. She had already been interviewed for *Woman's Own* some years previously, and also for *Out of the Dolls House*. She was one of the last surviving suffragettes.

"Why I was a suffragette: the need for education for women, and because white slave traffic was very prevalent, particularly in Bristol, being a port. Girls were kidnapped and never heard of again. The suffragettes wanted the vote – they were told the time was not ripe.

181

Only a handful of women alive today remember being behind bars for their part in the suffrage campaign. Victoria Lidiard is one of the last of a tough breed. At ninety-six, she manages her roomy Brighton flat entirely on her own, her respectable neighbours little suspecting that in her youth this sprightly and pleasant retired optician did time in Holloway. Yet in 1912 Victoria was gaoled for two months for taking part in one of Emmeline Pankhurst's days of action. At a pre-arranged time, suffragettes smashed windows all over central London. Victoria's beat was Whitehall; her target the War Office. She looked as demure as possible, deliberately walking in step with a policeman to allay suspicion. When she suddenly threw a stone through one of the War Office windows, the policeman could not believe his eyes. 'He just looked at me. Meantime another policeman rushed up towards me and then an inspector on horseback came. So I was escorted to Bow Street, a policeman each side of me, clutching my arm, and one behind. Well, I had eight stones, but I'd only used one (unlike Mrs Pankhurst who was renowned for her inaccuracy, Victoria was a good shot) so on the way to the police station I dropped them one by one and to my amazement when I was taken down at Bow Street, this policeman that had followed put the seven stones on the table and said, "She dropped these on the way." ' The case against her was complete.

3 GENERATIONS

One woman is 99 years old—she was a suffragette who fought for the right to vote for us all. The other is just 18, she's about to vote for the first time and has opportunities women never dreamed of 60 years ago. So what do they have in common? Victoria Freedman reports. Main picture by Alistair Morrison

Victoria Lidiard is white haired, very hard of hearing and walks slowly and with difficulty. She's 99 years old but the minute she begins to speak there's no doubt that her mind is as quick as ever and the convictions and opinions she had as a young woman are still strong. The same fierce determination that made her a suffragette in the early part of the century is still very much present.

Seated next to her is 18-year-old Margaret Noak. She's just taken three A-levels and intends to go to college to study technology. It would have been unthinkable in Mrs Lidiard's day. But thanks to the pressure brought by the suffragettes at a time when a woman's place was in the home and not out campaigning and fighting in the streets, Margaret—and millions of other young women like her—has choices and opportunities which Mrs Lidiard only dreamed of.

These two women have grown up in completely different worlds. Margaret takes it for granted that she will vote in the next election—for Mrs Lidiard that was an achievement she devoted most of her life to fighting for.

Mrs Lidiard is proud of what women are achieving now but she's also impatient with those who don't push hard enough to follow up her victories. And Margaret is fascinated by just how a young woman could have found the courage 80 years ago to stand up and fight against the government and the disapproval of society. So we decided to bring them together to talk about their lives, what they feel women have achieved—what they've lost and what they should still be fighting for.

Mrs Lidiard, her mother and five sisters joined the suffragette movement in 1910. She was 21 years old, and was immediately convinced she should join after hearing Annie Kenney, a leading suffragette, address a meeting.

"There were two main reasons why I joined. Firstly, girls didn't have an education like boys did. Girls went to schools where they learned how to *behave*," she says with distaste. "The other reason was the white slave traffic. I didn't know anything about it until I came into contact with the suffragette movement and I found out that nicely brought up girls were being abducted and sold as slaves."

In no time Mrs Lidiard was an active member, selling the paper

Fighting for rights: 80 years ago dedicated suffragettes campaigned against bitter hostility and prejudice so that women could have the right to vote

Votes for Women and attending meetings, listening to leaders like Emmeline Pankhurst and her daughter Christabel urging women to take up the cause.

"The meetings were never advertised in the papers, so quite a number of us would go out about seven in the morning and chalk the time and place on the pavement. I remember one morning, I'd nearly finished, and I saw a policeman coming round the corner, so I ran and jumped on a tram.

"But he caught up, and arrested me. I was let off with a caution and warned not to do it again—but of course I did," she says, smiling at the astonished look she gets from Margaret, who can't imagine doing anything like that now, let alone at the beginning of the century when women were still in long dresses and corsets.

It was revolutionary behaviour even by today's standards, but the suffragettes risked their lives and their freedom for the cause. They

chained themselves to railings, caused damage to buildings and one, Emily Davison, died after throwing herself in front of the King's horse on Derby Day 1913.

Mrs Lidiard herself was sent to prison, two years after joining the movement. "Mrs Pankhurst said that women who did things for the movement wouldn't have to hunger strike," she tells Margaret. "My mother wouldn't let me go on hunger strike, so one Monday I went to Whitehall. There were police everywhere, but they let me through and I went and stood right next to a policeman and threw a stone through a Home Office window!" she says, still pleased at her nerve.

"He looked at me in surprise— he didn't think I could have done it. But another policeman a little further on thought I wasn't so innocent as I looked, so he dashed up, grabbed my right arm, the other policeman grabbed my left arm, another one rode up on a horse and there was another one at the back,

and they all escorted me to Bow Street Police Station.

"I still had seven more stones in my pocket, so as I went along dropped them casually one by one But the policeman behind me picked them up, and when we got to the police station he pulled them out of his pocket and told the officer in charge that I'd dropped them on the way. That was very mean of him wasn't it?" she says with the smile of a naughty child.

The next day Mrs Lidiard appeared at Bow Street Court and was sentenced to two months' hard labour. She was taken to Holloway Prison and put in an "observation" cell. "It was partly underground with plain walls and a door with iron bars. I remember the warden saying she was sorry to have to put me there and that she'd move me the next day.

"We were considered political prisoners and treated different from the ordinary ones. They used to come and wash our cells—they liked to do it as we'd talk to them because they weren't allowed to talk in Holloway. You know, I don't remember much of the whole time I was there, so I think it must have been a very traumatic experience.

But Mrs Lidiard didn't let her imprisonment stop her campaigning for women's right to vote. "Mrs Pankhurst always said the government would never move unless you pushed it, so push collectively and push hard."

Emmeline Pankhurst, whose name is a byword for the suffragette movement, inspired and motivated women all over Britain and Mrs Lidiard quotes her constantly. She heard her talk but I never actually met her," she says.

"She was a very religious woman—we all knew that. There was an atmosphere of serenity about her and very few people have that. She wasn't a violent woman at all. She said we were not to hurt anybody any way."

Margaret, who has been listening intently and with obvious admiration for the suffragettes' and Mrs Lidiard's extraordinary courage, can't imagine doing anything quite so daring.

"I think I'd do it for the same cause," she says. "Women getting the vote was a very big issue, but I can't think of anything nowadays that I'd go quite that far for."

"But you'd get so much more help these days," says Mrs Lidiard. For the suffragettes fought against

THE GREAT LANDMARKS

1867—first petition presented to Parliament asking for equal voting rights for women

1903—Mrs Emmeline Pankhurst founds the Women's Social and Political Union, later known collectively as the Suffragettes

1918—vote given to women but only if you were 30 or more

1919—Lady Astor, first woman MP

to take up her seat in Parliament

1928—the "flapper vote"—women aged 21 and over allowed to vote, in line with men

1970—Equal Pay Act came into force

1975—Sex Discrimination Act becomes law

1979—Margaret Thatcher becomes Britain's first woman Prime Minister

A songbird in Holloway

Victoria Lidiard

SUFFRAGETTE, lifelong campaigner for the ordination of women priests, and a vegetarian for over 90 years, Victoria Lidiard has died aged 102. She was one of the last surviving suffragettes, and like many others, did time in Holloway.

Answering Mrs Pankhurst's call to protest at the Liberal government's refusal to give women the vote, she went up to London from her home in Clifton, Bristol, and was one of 200 women who were arrested for smashing windows on March 4, 1912. She served two months for breaking a window at the War Office: "I went and stood near a policeman and threw a stone through an office win-

The young suffragette in 1910

dow. The policeman next to me looked at me, he couldn't believe that I'd done it . . . then I was led to Bow Street.

"There was a policeman on horseback in front, a policeman behind him, then me with one on each side of me and one at the back . . . I had eight stones and I had only used one, and so going back to Bow Street police station I dropped them one by one. When I arrived at Bow Street the policemen had picked them up. I thought that was particularly mean."

In recent years Victoria Lidiard did not remember very much about the time she spent in Holloway: "The [cell] windows were high up and if you wanted to look out of the window you had to stand on a chair — I used to stand there and sing out of the window at the top of my voice . . . I do remember having a black beetle in my porridge."

When she became a suffragette in 1907 she was a young, single, middle-class woman involved in the Women's Social and Political Union. Her mother and three of her four sisters also joined. She had learned shorthand and book-keeping and worked in photographic studios in Margate and Clifton. One day while selling the weekly paper Votes For Women, a local clergyman spat in her face in disgust. Drunks and young boys hurling abuse and rotten fruit were a hazard when she spoke at street-corner meetings.

Victoria Lidiard was 25 when the first world war broke out. She moved to London with one of her sisters and ran a guesthouse in Kensington, and at weekends worked in a Battersea munitions factory.

She was married in 1918 to a major in the Fifth Manchester Rifles. They had met when she was selling Votes For Women: he was an active sympathiser, a member of the Men's Political Union for Women's Enfranchisement, and had twice been thrown out of political meetings he had inter-

Victoria Lidiard . . . Campaigning for women   PHOTOGRAPH: JOHN CHASE

rupted — on one occasion landing up in a pond.

After the war Victoria Lidiard studied at the London Refraction Hospital at the Elephant and Castle and became their first woman staff refractionist in 1927. Eventually she and her husband, who was also an optician, opened a practice together in Maidenhead and another in High Wycombe.

"Many, many laws have been passed affecting women and children which would not have been passed unless women had the vote," she believed. Access to education had been the single biggest improvement in women's lives in her lifetime.

Right up to the end she campaigned for the ordination of women.

She drew parallels between the two campaigns which had played such a big part in her life. Recently, she remembered: "The opposition to the ordination of women is just the same opposition we fought for the vote. They could not reason. I don't mind people giving reasons, but not stupid prejudices."

Diane Atkinson

Victoria Lidiard, born December 27, 1889; died October 3, 1992

John Chase's photographs of Victoria Lidiard appear in the exhibition Purple, White And Green: Suffragettes in London, 1906-1914, at the Museum of London until June, 1993.

Pankhurst said, 'The government will not move unless you push them.' I am still a suffragette at heart!"

"We were eight children in the family. My father did not believe in education for girls; the money had to be spent on the boys. Girls did not get a decent education. Yet who wants to marry a fool? As girls did not get a good education before the vote was won, my sisters and I went to many evening classes. I do remember the first woman doctor, a gynaecologist, who started in Clifton. My mother wished to go and see her, but my father did not think it was possible for a woman to be capable of the work of a medical person. My mother's friend took her."

"I have seen *My Weekly*, *Home Chat*, *Vogue*. Not *The Englishwoman*. I do remember two magazines – one was *The Strand*, in which I read nearly all Sherlock Holmes before I was fifteen years old. Also *Tit Bits*. Thank you for sending me a copy of *Tit Bits*. Seeing it now I am not surprised it went west – it did not keep up with the times. Women still have a long way to go..."

"We did not go out a lot but had many social evenings at home – singing or talking. We all learnt to play chess and billiards, and were encouraged to read. There were lots and lots of books about. While as a family (large) we went to many good concerts at the Colston Halls, Bristol, we never went to a theatre. In those days actresses were not considered to be 'nice' people. Amusements were usually at home; when friends visited we enjoyed the evenings. While we had many friends they were somewhat restricted in number because people were apt to keep themselves to themselves."

"I was twenty-four at the beginning of the war. My sister and I ran a professional women's club. They were a nice lot of educated women. I worked at weekends in the munitions factory with my sister in Battersea. We took over on Sundays to let those working during the week have a rest. I did no other war work. My husband was in the army, though I was not married until 1918. I did knit socks, but was not patriotic personally. My husband and I were consultant opticians after the war."

MARGARET:

Margaret was ninety-eight when interviewed at her home in Hendon.

"I worked at Woolwich Arsenal all through the war at the Royal Army Ordnance Depot. I was directed there. I was called up. I spent most of the war loading shells on to railway trucks, and packing them onto the trucks and the railway lines. I was living in a hostel. I did both day and night work. There was a lot going on. One night, an airship came over, went right over the factory. The lights went out. Just before the end of the war they transferred us to Greenford."

Margaret remembered the magazines a little. She liked the pictures on the cigarette cards, remembered them.

"They remind me of my uniform at the Woolwich – khaki hat, coat, trousers for climbing to put shells into trucks, and puttees. I wound the puttees round at the front, they came out at the back. A young fellow from the RAF said, 'Come into my office and I'll show you how to fold them over.'"

The Hall Caine book delighted her and brought back many memories. "At first, women in the streets did not like to see us in uniform when the boys were fighting. Then they realised what we were doing. When I look back on it! At night, we were so tired we used to lie on the ammunition, it could have blown us all up. We used to write notes to the men in the trenches, and put them into the ammunition. I wrote to one man for a long time, but suddenly his letters stopped; he must have been killed."

"In the TNT sheds they blew up if a match was dropped. One girl dropped some, and the whole shed was blown up, and they were all killed. It was all kept quiet. I had to wear a mask. We *had* to do war work. Planes often came over. We had fun between whiles. We had a good time at Woolwich. The RAF were at the back, and soldiers. There were dances. We had a jolly good time."

"My first boyfriend wanted to get married before going to the Front. Then he wanted to get married at Christmas, while on leave. I refused – then he got killed. My brother was fighting in France. My father would not let me go, though I wanted to. When I look back – the things I used to do: mad! Got on a tram one morning to go to work. I went up to the front and said, 'I can drive this.' 'Come on then.' He let me drive all the way to Abbey Wood."

"When the war finished I wanted to get married. My father refused to let me – he said my husband was not well enough. We still got married. We were married a fortnight; he was ill all the time. After a fortnight, he fell in the door. I thought he was drunk. He had malaria, dysentery, had been gassed and shot in the back. My husband was ill for a long time. My first child, a little girl, was bonny until eleven months, then died. Then I had a boy – I shouldn't have had him really. When I visited my husband in hospital he showed me his wound – it had paper on it. There were no drugs or anything. I said, 'Come home, don't stop here.' A few days later at home, there was a rat-a-tat on the door, my little boy, Vincent, went to answer it: 'It's Daddy.' He had just walked out of the hospital. I went back. Sister 'carried on': 'What are you going to live on?' Our savings had all gone. I saw the Lady Almoner, told her I was tearing up sheets for the wound. 'Come on Fridays, I will give you 7s 6d and dressings.' I wanted to keep him at home. I went to work every morning for Lady C. I was so tired, no sleep, the smell of the wound all the time. I was half asleep when I got there. The head housemaid told me to go and have a sleep on the bed. Lady C's daughter wanted to see me, so I went to the drawing room. 'You should not be doing this wound. Go and get some incense from the chemist.' The smell was awful. I could not go on like that. 'It is not fair to your little boy.' She paid for a taxi for him to go back to hospital. There were no drugs. I went to the pub every day to get a drop of brandy for him to ease the pain. In three months he had wasted away."

189

MARGARET'S FULL STORY

I was born on the 15th August in the year 1893 in a little village in Sussex - Hadlow Down, near Buxted. My mother was a farmer's daughter in the village of Burwash. My father was the baker in Hadlow Down, and my mother kept the shop and sold sweets and bread. I was about three years old when I started going out with my Dad in the horse and cart to sell bread in the village. When I was about four years old, my dad bought a large shop in Tunbridge Wells. My people were living in Tunbridge Wells, and I went to school at St. James.

In my six weeks' holiday I went to stay at my mother's home, a farmhouse in Burwash, and sometimes to my Great Grandma's farm at Burwash Wheel. My Uncle Charlie would meet me at the station and then we would walk over twenty one fields to the farmhouse. It was a lovely farm, with lots of chickens, ducks, pigs and a lovely big haystack, which my cousins climbed into and sometimes slept right on the top of. I used to feed the chickens, and one thing I can remember, even now: the poor old duck was lying on eight eggs, but then she died, so my Uncle put a chicken on them. When they hatched out the ducks were only very little, but they got into the pond, and the poor old chicken was on the bank crying, because she could not swim.

At night I sometimes used to lie up in the loft and watch the hops being brought into the Oast house to be put in the large pot, or sacks to be pressed down to be sent to the brewers. We always had good food. My uncle used to shoot pigeons and rabbits for pies.

When we went to Great Grandmother's, it was very good, but she was very strict. The dairy was at the side of the house. I can remember sitting at a big table; there were oil lamps on the table, and I had to read from a big Bible. I always remember, it was the first chapter of St. John. I used to read it very quickly, and my Great Grandmother said, "Now my girl, you can read that again, and do not gabble this time".

Monday was "wash day", but before we could start on the clothes, we had to do all the washing up, which was left from the Sunday, because the only things we were allowed to wash up were the tea cups and saucers. We got up very early to light the "copper".

Tuesday was "ironing day". Wednesday was the day all the housework was done. Thursday was the day we put all the cream into the Vat and had to sit on the top to stop the lid coming off. It made a funny noise "slop,slop,slop". Then I used to help turn the handle, then we made it into "butter pats".

The thing I hated most was sleeping in my Grandmother's bed. I remember it was very high, so I had to be lifted into it, and then Grandmother closed all the curtains around the bed.

My uncle used to make coffins in the big shed. He died when I was eighteen. He left two boys and one girl. But Grandmother was still alive. I always remember seeing the coffins carried to the family plot. But my mother was not buried there. She went to Tunbridge Wells when she died. She was only 46.

Then my father had to leave the Bakery because of the dust from the flour getting on to his chest. He bought a small holding and he made the table and chairs. When I was nineteen my mother died. She had appendicitis, the same as George V died of. I looked after my brother - he was seventeen - and my Dad.

I found out my Dad was going to the cemetery and there he met this woman who was visiting another grave. She was not a bad woman, but my brother could not get on with her. I could talk to her sometimes, and she said "I am not wanting to take your mother's place". But my brother just did not like her, so he got married.

When I was fourteen I went into service, but when I was nineteen the First World War came, and I was called up into the Army, to Kings Norton, in Abbeywood, the Royal Army Ordnance Corps. We had to pack 4½ inch, 18 pounder shells, and put them into railway trucks to send them to the troops in France. Whilst there, in the factory, we formed a guard for King George V, Queen Mary and the Princess Royal.

I remember the first Zeppelin coming right over the factory, and dropping some bombs on some houses in Erith. I remember seeing a sugar factory being blown up in the middle of the night, one night when I was at work. We did one week nights, one week days.

When the war finished, two of my friends went to the Palace as house maids. I had met a soldier in the factory. I married him when he was discharged. My dad tried to get me to wait because he had been shot, but we would not. I had only been married a fortnight and he was ill with malaria and dysentery.

Oh! I forgot. I also remember the night a Zeppelin went over us and fell on a house. Three little girls were killed.

I had a little baby girl. She was bonny until she was eleven months old, when she was taken ill. I took her to Great Ormond Street Hospital. The doctors said she had got her disease from her dad because he was a soldier. She lost all her strength and she was gone.

My husband's two sisters went to work at Lyons Corner House in Oxford Street, London. His eldest sister married a Jewish boy, and he in those days was the "toy king" of the East End of London, before there was "Woolworths". The other sister met her husband in the Corner House. He was with the Dutch East India Company, working with oil. They went out to Sumatra and were there four years. There she had maids. Later they went to Holland, then to New Zealand. When they retired they went to Holland, but then Hitler came one night, and they caught the last ship to England.

We carried on married, and I had a little boy. He was about three years old when his Dad said he was in so much pain because his wound was hurting. So I took him to the West Middlesex Hospital. I spoke to a Doctor "Web Johnson" and he told me the army had been treating him for piles, but he had cancer. He said if he had seen him before he could have saved him. He put him in hospital. I went to see him and was upset; they only put paper on his wound. I said "You should come home". The next morning, my son and I were in bed, it was about 7 o'clock, when I heard a knock on the door. My son jumped out of bed, saying "Daddy". He had walked out of the hospital.

I went along and saw the lady Almoner, and things were bad. We had both saved all through the war, but we had to draw it out and his pension was only 7s 6d per week (35p). So the hospital told me to go up on Friday and they would give me sheets to cover his wound, because his back passage was on his side, and I cleaned the wound. I had to go to the chemist and get a roll of disinfected lint, and every time I did his wound I had to burn it, to kill the smell. He did not go to bed. I cut a hole in a cane armchair and put a potty around it, and he used it, and he used to sleep there, but he was in awful pain. There were no drugs to relieve him, I used to go and get him a small drop of whisky.

I went to work in the mornings. I remember I was so tired when I went one morning, and the housemaid made me go on her bed. That morning I was working for Lady Templemore, in Cambridge Terrace, for three hours, and her daughter asked where I was. She called me into the drawing room and said "This cannot go on". She talked to me and told me that the cancer would touch the bladder. I went home one morning and it had, so they got him in Castle Bellfield, in the Catholic hospital, and he was there three months, when he died.

I carried on with my son, and got a job as housekeeper with a Miss Bathurst-Norman at Notting Hill. I paid a neighbour to mind my son.

Another neighbour who had got friendly with my husband, one night said "Do not be in a hurry"; so we became friends and got married.

Then when our house was knocked down we came to live in Burnt Oak. He used to walk to Cricklewood garage, because he worked on the No.1 bus.

Then the Second World War came. I began to get ill; I went down to 7 stone, and had to leave my job. I was having a job with my boy. I came home and could not find him; I was paying a neighbour to look after him. I found him near the water getting tiddlers out of the water. I was so worried, so Lady Wellesday said "bring him down to the country cottage, near Littlehampton". If I got him down there she would get him into the Convent. She got him in there because I promised his Dad I would bring him up a Catholic.

I was crying on the train, and she was very good. She brought me a large glass of milk, and said she would always go and see him. I went down to 7 stone, it was the bother with my boy. We left Cottesmore to go into Rustington. He was in the Convent for four years.

I was so scared when my heart used to pump, pump, my Doctor gave me Morphine, and said I must rest. My husband brought me in ½ a bottle of port and ½ a bottle of Guinness and said I was to take ½ a wine glass in the morning and half a glass in the afternoon. I went back to the Doctor. He said I was looking much better. I said "It was not your Morphine, but the port and the guinness". So he said "You had better go back and take some more."

My friend used to come in and help me dress, because I was so weak. I was so fed up by myself, my husband said "You had better bring the boy home, because you miss him so much." I did not have much money because I could not have a War Pension for my first husband, because he died twelve months after the War. But a Major Tyron fought Whitehall, and got me a Widows' Pension; it was 10 shillings.

Then they pulled our house down and sent us to Edgware. That was near my husband's garage at Cricklewood. My husband was trying to get my nerves back, he told me the doctor said not to give into me. He was good - he would come out with me as I would not cross the Edgware Road then. We had notice that our house was going to be pulled down, Park West was to be built there. They offered us a house at Burnt Oak, and as my husband was a bus driver at Cricklewood garage, this enabled him to walk home when he was on late turn. So we moved there. About six years later the Second World War came. We were right at the back of Hendon Aerodrome, and would see the planes going up.

193

My youngest boy and I used to go into the dugout and wait for Dad to come home. When the sirens went off, these foolish pilots used to fly off in their planes. We had a bomb drop at the top of the garden in Thirby Road, but "thank God" all the people who were there were in the dugout; but the houses were all down.

Then the War finished, and my husband retired. We had a few happy years together, and then he had 'flu, which knocked his heart, then he died and the Welfare lady said she would get me into Deansbrook Day Centre. I have been there just on eight years and very happy there. Everyone has been so good.

My eldest son was at Stag Lane working at Dehavilland's on aircraft. He came in one morning and said he was going to finish, as he had been 6 months on nights, and they would not put him on days. I tried to make him see sense, but he laughed and went into the Army, and after a few months he was sent to Africa. He went to the invasion of Sicily and also Italy.

He was posted missing, but the Red Cross found him in a Hospital there, and they sent him home on a hospital ship to Scotland. When the hospital closed they sent him down to the hospital in Shenley, the military part of Shenley. He had an operation on his head, but it left him with fits. Then he began to get better, and the Doctor said he could come home at weekends. This he did, and then one Monday the police from Hendon came and told me to get in touch with the hospital. They in turn told me he had died in the night. He had been home on the Sunday - it was a shock that my boy, who had only been home that weekend before, had died.

CONCLUSION

The Comfort Factor:

"It was an escape as things were difficult. The information was useful on fashion, health, recreation, ideas for the home. The fiction was a fantasy world – the stories always ended happily."

The impact of social change on the medium of women's magazines is a complex issue. It concerns how, in what ways, and by whom its messages have changed over time, and the relationship between the historical context and what was shown in the magazines. Since the 1950s, the supporting, reinforcing 'we women' approach of these magazines has been manifested through journalistic techniques such as 'writespeak', personalising a *consciously classless* social structure which they project through their titles: *Woman, Woman's Own*, etc. Prior to this period, the titles were more personalised, with less use of the all-enveloping feminine gender: *My Weekly, Home Chat, Peg's Paper*, and so on. There are, of course, exceptions in both periods; more 'upmarket' titles – *Vogue, Queen, The Lady, The Englishwoman*, and so forth. Many of the messages seem to have changed since the Second World War but many remain the same, in spite of the changes in women's lives. There now appears to be a sudden surge in publishing magazines which are very similar to those in the 1950s. Whereas the magazines of the 1960s focused much more on glamour, magazines such as *Best, Essentials, Me*, as well as the continuing *Woman, Woman's Own, Woman's Weekly*, are full of features on sewing, cooking, etc. again.

The editors' belief in 'shared consciousness' forms the basis of publishing rationale; it rises above individual economic, social and personality differences, and provides a basis for solidarity.

Yet this solidarity produces its own dilemma: the need to recognise, react to or lead social change; to gather in the multiple strands of external influence and find a mix within which constancy and change are interwoven. Supportive, understanding and reinforcing purposes must remain a constant even if the subjects or circumstances change.

However, as we have seen, the gap between the context of the magazine and the 'lifestyle' of the reader is considerably wider than is apparent from a study of the magazines alone. In particular, the experiences of the women who lived through the First World War did not filter through to the magazines; nor did magazine editors attempt to transfer or transform these experiences into features or fiction which could then be relayed to their readers. As Sybil, one of the interviewees, suggested: "They dealt with the *consequences* of the war – how to make an eggless cake, etc." Editorial policy still defines the ways in which their followers should think, and what they should say, do, wear, cook, read, explore, ignore and care about. The *basic message* remains: the premise of biological predestination, gender determinism, and the 'woman to woman' approach. On the surface, the range of roles and expectations has widened beyond the earlier emphasis on romance, marriage and the 'waiting to wed girl'. The roles of 'wife' and 'mother', however, remain permanent in the magazines, which have continued using the same format, and which are still reaching out to the 'same' reader, even when joined by the new 'independent' woman. *Overtly*, she is urged to achieve her full potential outside the home as well as within it. *Covertly*, she carries within her the cultural image of the wife and mother of previous generations, whom she is still expected to replicate. The message is pointing in two directions: 1. 'Set out and show the world you are someone within your own right' and 2. 'Remember you must achieve as a wife and mother too'. The resulting psychological tension generated is largely ignored, and the package is overlaid with a seductive wrapping – every woman can 'choose' the 'kind of woman she wishes to be'.

The message still continues to be that women are uniquely different, and require separate treatment and instruction in ways that men do not. Man remains the goal, as possession of a male partner confers prestige within the female world; even in the magazines which appear to be representing the 'modern' woman, with all the connotations this image calls to mind.

From this continuing policy within the magazines it would seem difficult to define their relevance to women's changing experience of social life. They have been dismissed as, at best, superficial and trivial publications; as at worst a commercial exploitation to sell women all and sundry. Even those who find them both useful and pleasurable may hesitate to admit to this, in case of scorn. They are seen also as *ephemeral* publications, often read with only half an eye and only partly digested before being discarded – and only remembered with difficulty:-

"Life did not change during the war. I did nothing for the war effort. I did not read magazines – too busy."
(Joan)

"I had no spare time for reading – could not afford magazines on 3s 4d a week wages."
(Ethel)

"I was not affected by what I read in the magazines."
(Sybil)

"I was one of a large family, did not have time to read."
(Jane)

It would seem that what is read does, to a large extent, pass without remembrance, and this is largely confirmed by the points of view of the 'witnesses'. Only when *shown* the magazines did they recall the titles, or titles of other magazines which were not available.

Yet it is now believed that the mass media – which includes this type of publication – *do* influence audiences: not by sudden opinion change, but by the gradual accumulation of beliefs and values. Collective representations can hold social groups together, and women's magazines provide a useful example of this. They have always had an important *socialising* function, particularly when aimed at working class women as guides to 'how life should be lived'. Therefore it is important that this seemingly trivial cultural form is understood, questioned and challenged as a political issue.

The magazines both reflect and dismiss social changes, or try to reinforce the continuity of the cult of 'femininity' and the need to reinforce whatever the 'status quo' of the historical period happens to be. Their influence on their readers has, therefore, to be so subtle as to go almost unnoticed, particularly in long term memory. They record change, and gradually incorporate it, yet reinforce and try constantly to revamp and revitalise underlying ideological patterns in order to retain the structure. Their readers subconsciously accept the changes offered to them, as well as the reiteration of continuing

197

symbols – as far as it is possible to tell. From the readers' point of view, it would seem that they continue to need the psychological reassurance of a middle class world; of being able vicariously to feel they are part of that world and that it is still there, as it has always been. Particularly, there is the acceptance of the fiction, the enjoyment of reading about a world they can never inhabit and often which has never really existed. The *comfort* factor is a very important one, and reiterates the enjoyment of 'escapism'.

The magazines offered a continuity in troubled times, a 'home front' security. In actual fact, the two world wars seemed to be fused together, from the point of view of the 'witnesses', as a 'wartime' separate from everyday life, and this brought the memory of the magazines to the fore even more strongly, as part of that security; something that was always 'there'. Sybil, as well as several of the other interviewees, was very aware of this repetitive security:-

> "It was an escape as things were difficult. The information was useful on fashion, health, recreation, ideas for the home. The fiction was a fantasy world – the stories always ended happily."

In the magazines, as in the literature of the period, there was no real mention of the horrors of war, only articles and stories based on patriotism, the war effort, and stoicism. The novelists could only look back in revealing their experiences after the reality, when it could be evaluated, as the pain had lessened a little. Some of the 'witnesses' felt the same way – one or two refused to be interviewed about the war, as even seventy-five years later it was too painful to talk about.

On the 17th January, 1991, war broke out in the Middle East between Iraq and the USA, Britain, France and other members of the United Nations. The Allied Forces now contain many more women, playing roles that would have been unthinkable in 1914; working alongside their male companions, taking part in the same training, though stopping short of actual combat. In physical and psychological terms the women *have* gone to war, in many cases kissing their husbands and children goodbye.

At home, once again, parents, wives, children and sweethearts play the waiting game. On television and in the newspapers, pride in their loved ones is overlaid with fear and loneliness; there is, fortunately, more open discussion of their inability to cope with the possibility of loss and injury than of the need to win the war:

> "Julie talks with a certain trepidation about her life as the wife of one of the Navy's brightest young officers in the Gulf War. 'But I feel as if we wives were waging a war of our own...'
>
> 'Before he had left for the Gulf, he had made his will.' They had discussed how she would live her life if he died... Friends were kind, and said they understood. But how could they? She went round in a daze, watching people doing their shopping and knowing that then, because it was a 'media' war, they could switch on their television in the evening and say, 'Oh, how's it going today?'
>
> 'I see an aggression in him that I never saw before. Sleepless nights are spent trying to come to terms with the knowledge that he has actually had to kill people.'" (From an interview in *The Guardian*, 1991).

There is also, now, more open discussion of PTSD: combat-related Post Traumatic Stress Disorder. Horacio Benitez is an Argentinian veteran from the Falklands War. He states that, "The worst feeling that stays with you after the war is a terrible guilt. You ask yourself how many fathers you may have killed. And you ask yourself 'Why?' *The Guardian* of September, 1991, discussed this modern recognition, noting that this mainly privately suffered torment is a malignant condition of delayed stress. "Unrecognised (as it was at the time of the First World War), it can wreak havoc among soldiers and their families, manifesting as irrational rages, domestic violence, drug-taking and alcoholism, flashbacks, nightmares, and numerous suicides."

There is now a Gulf Families Crisis Line, recently given support on television by Terry Wogan, but, so far, receiving very little help from the Ministry of Defence or the British Army.

Yet, in the magazines, no mention of the war found its way into the pages until the 2nd February 1991 issue of *Hello!*, in which the front cover offers a photograph of a woman manning a machine gun on a tank with the headline: "Brave women who make a vital contribution to the war effort fighting on the Gulf front line":-

> "For many years now women have played a vital role in the services but in the last couple of weeks the vivid photographs of uniformed women, equipped with machine guns and expertly handling very sophisticated combat machinery, dramatically dispel the old image of the Florence Nightingale type figure nursing the wounded back to health."

Perhaps, at last, the world of the magazines and that of reality are beginning to merge.

HELLO!

NUMBER 138 • FEBRUARY 2, 1991 • £1

GOLDEN GLOBE WINNER
JULIA ROBERTS
TALKING ABOUT HER
LOVE FOR HER MAN

BRAVE WOMEN WHO MAKE A VITAL CONTRIBUTION TO THE WAR EFFORT FIGHTING ON THE GULF FRONT LINE

LIST OF WORKS CONSULTED

1. Carol ADAMS, *Ordinary Lives* (London: Virago Press Ltd, 1984).

2. Richard ALDINGTON, *Death of a Hero* (London: Hogarth Press, 1984).

3. John BERGER, *Ways of Seeing* (Penguin Books, 1979).

4. Gail BRAYBON and Penny SUMMERFIELD, *Out of the Cage* (London: Pandora Press, 1987).

5. Vera BRITTAIN, *Testament of Youth* (London: Virago Press Ltd, 1978).

6. Mary CADOGAN and Patricia GRAY, *Women and Children First* (London: Victor Gollancz Ltd, 1971).

7. Hall CAINE, *Our Girls* (London: Hutchinson and CO., 1917).

8. James CURRAN, Angus DOUGLAS, Garry WHANNEL, 'The Political Economy of the Human-Interest story' in A SMITH, *Newspapers & Democracy*.

9. Marjorie FERGUSON, *Forever Feminine* (London: Heinemann, 1983).

10. Ford Madox FORD, *Parade's End* (Penguin Books, 1988).

11. Bridget FOWLER, *Popular Fiction and Social Change*, ed. Christopher PAWLING, (London: Macmillan Press, 1984).

12. Radclyffe HALL, *The Well of Loneliness* (London: Virago Press Ltd, 1985).

13. Angela HOLDSWORTH, *Out of the Dolls House* (BBC Books, 1988).

14. Terry JORDAN, *Agony Columns 1890-1980* (Optima; Macdonald & Co. (Publishers) Ltd, 1988).

15. Robin KENT, *Aunt Agony Advises* (London: WH Allen, 1979).

16. D.H. LAWRENCE, *Kangaroo* (Penguin Books, 1976).

17. *'The Changing Experience of Women'*, Unit 6, Femininity and Women's Magazines, Open University 2nd Level Course, (OU Press, Walton Hall, Milton Keynes, MK7 6AA).

18. Irene RATHBONE, *We That Were Young* (London: Virago Books, 1988).

19. Janice A RODWAY, *Reading the Romance* (London and Chapel Hill: University of Carolina Press, 1984).

20. Helen Zenna SMITH, *Not So Quiet* (London: Virago Press Ltd, 1988).

21. 'Mass Media' in *Society Today, New Society*, 21 November 1988.

22. Diana SOUHAINE, *A Woman's Place: The Changing Picture of Women in Britain* (Penguin Books, 1986).

23. Marina WARNER, *Monuments and Maidens* (London: Weidenfeld and Nicholson, 1985).

24. Rebecca WEST, *The Return of the Soldier* (London: Virago Press Ltd, 1987).

25. Janice WINSHIP, *Inside Women's Magazines* (London: Pandora Press, 1987).

26. Virginia WOOLF, *Mrs Dalloway* (London: Granada Publishing Ltd, 1982).

27. * Arthur MARWICK, *Women at War 1914-1918,* (Fontana Original, Fontana Paperbacks, 1977).

28. *1914 Illustrated: The Book of the Year November 1913-November 1914,* The Daily News and Reader (Headley Bros, Bishopsgate, London, EC).

29. Peter LIDDLE, *Testimony of War, 1914-1918* (Michael Russell (Publishing) Ltd). The Chantry, Wilton, Salisbury, 1979).

30. ed. A.J.P. TAYLOR, *History of World War I* (Octopus Books Ltd, 59 Grosvenor Street, London, W1, 1974).

31. Carol TWINCH, *Women on the* Land (Lutterworth Press).

* With acknowledgements to
  The Trustees of the Imperial War Museum.

APPENDIX 1

QUESTIONNAIRE

Do you still read women's magazines?
Can you remember what you read when you were younger?
Here are some magazines produced in the period immediately before, during and after the First World War. I also have a list of other magazines which it has not been possible to obtain. Do these names mean anything to you?

1. Where were you living during World War I?

2. How old were you when the war started?

3. Were you married during the war?

4. Did you have a job in the war? Was this what you could have seen yourself doing before the war?

5. a. What was your job?
    b. How long did you do it for?
    c. Did you change jobs during the war?
    d   What was your *first* job during the war?
    e   What job did you change to?
    f   Was this change difficult?
    g. Did you enjoy what you did?

6. What sort of memories do these magazines conjure up?

7. What sort of memories do the names of the other magazines conjure up?

8. Under what circumstances did you obtain and read these magazines?

9. Why did you read them? For relaxation, information, escape, etc.?

10. What did you like best about the magazines? Was it the fashion, information about jobs, practical help towards the war effort, the advertisements, ideas for the home?

11. Do you remember the problem pages?
    a. Did you read these?
    b. Did any problem seem to apply to your situation?
    c. Did you ever write in with a problem?

12. Did you read all the fiction?

13. Was this a form of escapism for you?

14. Did you find the magazines very patriotic? Did they deal with the war, like the newspapers? What did they say about the war?

APPENDIX 2

WOMEN IN WARTIME:
THE ROLE OF WOMEN'S MAGAZINES 1914-1918

The majority of people do not recognise 'propaganda' as such. So, for women, 'giving them their freedom' worked remarkably in World War I, and equally well in World War II, until they saw that they had, to a large extent, to give it back. Yet they allowed themselves to be 'persuaded' to go back to domesticity again. Women's magazines seemed to reinforce this – and still do – with subtle changes according to current trends, changing standards, altered ideology, broadening horizons.

I feel it would be interesting to pose the following questions, by looking at the magazines of this period:-

1. How was the war presented to women? *very patriotic*

2. How were they *expected* to react? *do something for the war effort*

3. Did they really accept the sense of guilt which allowed them to persuade their menfolk to go and fight; for example, shown in the letters pages?

4. Is class difference obvious in the magazines? *no*

5. Is sexuality expressed or suppressed? What about sexual revolution? *suppressed*

6. Is 'femininity' reinforced – for when the 'heroes' return? *no*

7. Was women's *passive* role enforced until they were needed, because of casualties, to go into men's jobs? Did it appear that they would have no problems in 'taking over'? Did the tone of the magazines change obviously and suddenly? *no problem*

8.   Was their influence brought to bear re: the need for child care? – *yes*, infant welfare? – *yes*, increase in childbearing where possible? – was it class biased? – *no*

9.   Does the new sense of 'power' come through – the ability to *do*? *yes*

10. *Iconography* – in magazines – of women war workers, especially nurses. Maternal versus power, role reversal – was this shown through the articles and/or advertisements?

11. Were the magazines a 'forum for discussion' of important issues of the time? Did they look forward to women's *place* in post-war terms? *yes*

12. Did the *fiction* reflect the topical issues? *yes*

13. Did the magazines vary in approach – more or less narrow, serious or radical? *serious*

14. The letters pages and agony columns: were they as important a part of the magazines during the war as previously – *yes*, or post-war? How *real* did they appear? – *pretty good*

SYBIL

APPENDIX 3

STANDARD LETTER

Dear —,

I wonder whether any of your residents would be interested in talking to me about women's magazines during the period of the First World War. I am at present engaged in writing a dissertation as the final part of my M.A. at Hatfield Polytechnic. The M.A. course is entitled 'Literature in Crisis'. I have chosen to examine women's magazines during the period 1914-1918, in an attempt to record the social and cultural changes taking place at that time, and how they were reflected through the medium of the magazines.

In order to add a more personal touch to my dissertation, I feel it would be interesting to add some personal recollections, impressions and comments on the magazines by women, who may have read them. I realise that the period I have chosen precludes all but a very few women, as they would be over 90 years of age in order to have been in their late 'teens or early twenties during the war.

I have prepared a basic questionnaire (a copy of which is enclosed). I would not, of course, require or expect any personal information, but hope that by producing copies of one or two magazines it would be possible to jog memory and revive recollections of former reading pleasure – or irritation – and remembrance of the period in which they were produced.

If you feel any of your residents come within the age category, and might be interested in talking to me, I should be very pleased to meet them. If, however, you feel I am intruding on their privacy, I shall quite understand.